Responsive Academic Decision Making

Involving Faculty in Higher Education Governance

Edited by:

Dr. Michael T. Miller
Associate Professor and Chair
Higher Education Administration Program
University of Alabama

Stillwater, Oklahoma
U.S.A.

Copyright © 1999 by New Forums Press, Inc.
All rights reserved.

Printed in the United States of America.

Additional copies may be ordered from New Forums Press, Inc., P.O. Box 876, Stillwater, OK 74076; or by phone at (405) 372-6158. Visit our web site at www.newforums.com.

ISBN: 1-58107-020-9

Table of Contents

Foreword xi

Section 1: Considering The Co-Governance Issue 1

1. Conceptualizing Faculty Involvement
   in Governance. 3

   by Dr. Michael Miller, University of Alabama

   Leadership and Administration 4
   Modeling Involvement. 8
       Legislative Model 8
       Watch-Dog Model 10
       Ladder Approach 11
       Six Perceptions Model. 20
   The Research and Teaching Paradox 22
   Legal Parameters of Involvement 24
   For Discussion 27

2. Benefits and Barriers to Shared Authority 29

   by Dr. Jennifer P. Evans, University of Alabama

   Current State of Decision-Making 31
       Group Process and Communication 31
           Decision Making Process 31
           Communication 31
       Group Leadership 33
       Organizational Influences 34
       Keys to Success 35
   Struggle with Authentic vs. Inauthentic
   Employee Involvement 36
       Historical Perspective 36
           Classical Approach 36

Human Relations and Resources. 37
Contemporary Perspective 40
Evolution of an Ethical Organization. 41
Benefits to Shared Decision-Making 42
The Empowerment Issue 43
Empowerment and Risk Taking 43
Benefits in Academe 44
Contemporary Research on Faculty
Involvement 45
Empowering Faculty 46
Ideal Governance Process 47
Improving Organization Conditions for
Faculty Involvement 48
Change 48
Conflict Management 49
Communication Skills 50
Successful Meeting Skills 50
Time Management 51
For Discussion 52

Section 2: Faculty Co-Governance At Work 55

3. Faculty Involvement in Academic Affairs 57

by Dr. Michael Miller, University of Alabama, Dr. Richard Newman, Presbyterian College, and Mr. Todd Adams, University of Toledo

Who is Involved in Academic Governance? 59
President 59
Provost 60
Deans 62
Chairs 63
Program Coordinators 64
Issues and Trends 65
Authority and Accountability. 66
Budgeting 66

Tenure and Promotion 67
Evaluation 68
Program Management... 69
Student Affairs: An Academic Area? 71
    Purpose of Student Affairs Administration 71
    Student Affairs/Academic Affairs
        Dichotomy 72
    Faculty Involvement in Student Affairs 74
A Balancing Act.. 76
    The Empowerment Issue 76
    Trust and Mistrust... 77
    Communication and Propaganda 78
    Seeking Success 78
For Discussion 80

4. Faculty Involvement in Athletic Administration 81

    by Dr. Richard E. Newman, Presbyterian College and Ms. Jane G. Bartee, University of Alabama

Controlling College Sports 83
    Historical Control Measures 83
    Current Control Measures 87
Sharing Authority Effectively 89
    Positive Impacts of Faculty Involvement........ 89
    Non-Involvement Impacts 91
Involving Faculty: Methods for Collaboration 92
For Discussion 95

5. Faculty Involvement in Institutional Fund Raising 97
    by Dr. Thomas A. Bila, Coffey, Bila, and Associates

Who Raises Money? 99
A Basic Fund Raising Philosophy 101
    Guiding Fund-Raising Principles 102
    Principles in Action 102

People Give to People 102
People Want Happy Experiences 103
People Want to Help 104
Partnerships May be Formed 104
Annual Giving Provides a Beginning 105
Trust is Developed Through
  Stewardship 106
Donors Expect Recognition 107
Involvement is Vital 108
Ninety Percent Comes from 10 percent .. 109
Donors Give Based on Interests 110
Involving Faculty in Development 111
For Discussion 112

Section 3: Making Use of the Shared Governance Process 115

6. Faculty Involvement in Evaluating Institutional Effectiveness and Planning 117

   by Dr. Thomas F. McCormack, Marion Military Institute, and Dr. Exir Brennen, Alabama A&M University

   Is There a Need to Change? 118
     Public Calls for Accountability 118
     Accrediting Agencies' Roles 119
     Federal and State Impetus 120
     Faculty Tradition and Ambition 120
   Changing from Within 122
     Measuring Effectiveness as Accountability 122
     To Do the Impossible 124
     Creating Distinctiveness 127
   For Discussion 128

7. Putting it all Together: Effective Faculty Governance .131

by Dr. Kathleen Randall and Dr. Michael Miller, University of Alabama

The Involved Faculty 131
Assessing Inclusive Decision-Making 132
For Administrators 135
   Administrative Strategies for Encouraging
   Communication and Citizenship 136
   Recognition Strategies for Enhancing
   a Shared Governance System 137
For Faculty 139
   Responsibility 139
   Democratic Ideals 140
   Integrity 140
   Role Definition 141
   Willingness to Lead 141
Visioning the Future of Involved Governance 142
For Discussion 145

References 147

Appendices 159
   Appendix 1: Letter of Faculty Appointment 161
   Appendix 2: Listing of Institutional Governance
                       Committees 163
   Appendix 3: Sample Administrator Rating 165
   Appendix 4: Pyramid Concept of Academic Alumni
                       Giving 167

Author Notes 169

Foreword

Perhaps educators find solace in Frost's poem "The Road Not Taken" because their research efforts have rendered little consensus in such strategic areas as governance. There appears to be only "slight" relief from the storm over how the profession is managed. Educators continue to seek the axiom that truth is the key to mastery, and mastery we have not in the management arena. These symbolic roads provide testing beds for concepts, to set aside and to develop. The task is to avoid the "fools gold" and continue the quest for truth, because in the process, concepts become reality. As Robert Levine indicated, symbolism at some juncture should be connected to reality, and as purveyors of the value of our product should know, we are in danger of overselling and creating an image of fraud.

Problems in education remain obvious in academic cultures beset with unique histories and practices that are difficult to dispel. People management within specific models and cultures are marred in the minds of those dictating processes and practices for the corporate structures. The product of these processes has not satisfied the public, either locally or nationally. Their opinions are based upon perceptions of poor management and a lack of agreement among responsible people. As Robert Birnbaum indicated "...it is time to look at new governance realities and to consider different paradigms for thinking about how institutional structures and interactions can be studied." The need to invoke better ways of doing business in this field is ever pressing. Although directed at education, the principles and concepts are applicable to most corporate structures.

Perceptions of higher education management are spawning at an alarming rate in and out of academe to the extent that those migrating in the profession may experience confusion and bewilderment. Little is sacrosanct, with opinions and interpretation jaded by writer and orator alike. Because the definition base shifted with the impact of relativism, there appears to be a grasping for firm consensus in specific areas of education. Anne Matthews in her book *Bright College Years: Inside The American Campus Today* portrays that the 'halls' are not secure, the curriculum is astray from perceived purposes. Is it, as she says, "a remarkably unwatched industry?" Are process and management the problem? Are committees vaporous and participants ubiquitous?

Where is consensus on the issues of institutional management? Price Pritchett indicated that methods matter as much as results. Put another way, he said, "How could the ends be considered excellent if we can't be proud of the means?" Such is the burden that educators bear in a profession where the two arms (administrators and faculty) of the structure are responsible for the input and output. What is the problem? Is it the decision or how the decision was made? Should the two arms exchange their fingers? If it were just that simplistic!

What process did educators bring to the table in their deliberation of those decisions affecting programs of remediation, changing traditional grading, distance learning, and academic credit for prior experiences? Are these the product of a consessus process agreed to as a method of improving the product? Or, to the contrary, do they conjure up the perceptions of unbridled internal processes within the management structure, with little regard for standards and interactions, and high regard for body count?

Funds always influence decision making, and historically, academic faculty have not played a strong role in the budgetary process. But the boding fact that the product is suspect stimulates the fault factor and need to place the blame. Educators cannot bypass the problem because of participation in the decision process. Education is everyone's business, regardless of whom makes the decisions. In this competitive society, a product of the education process is viewed in terms of the use, i.e., blue collar or white collar. Products from professional or technical training cultures are seen through functionality. Wayne Maher, manager of a coffee shop in Atlanta cannot fill vacant positions because most applicants cannot meet the requirements to fill out the application and list a home telephone number. As Maher says, "A worker who can't read an application form can't be trusted to read instructions." Will all the words about assessment and accountability provide an acceptable answer to Mr. Maher's question? What will satisfy "users" of products and "watchers" of processes may never be known! But, educators know that continuing confrontation within the educational cultures will only perpetuate the problem. Educators need to get their act together!

These writings provide a thematic examination of how faculty are involved in the governance process in different areas of higher education management. What is impressive about this collection, and the National Data Base on Faculty Involvement in Governance (NDBFIG) at The University of Alabama is the collegial and voluntary nature of participation. The Data Base was conceptualized in 1993 by a graduate student, Thomas McCormack, at The University of Alabama and Dr. Michael Miller, then at the University of Nebraska-Lincoln. Through a 1,000 mile friendship, these two individuals enlisted the support and help of their colleagues and friends, and built what has today become a data set of over 4,000 faculty ratings of governance activities. With 35 active colleges and universities participating in data collection activities, NDBFIG has also worked to promote shared governance, define and refine institutional effectiveness, and create an environment among faculty and administrators which encourages at the very least the discussion of how decisions should be made for the welfare of the campus.

Although this text offers different styles and tones in various chapters, the discussions of involvement in academic and student affairs, athletics, advancement, and institutional effectiveness and planning are helpful to all of those interested in a setting where group input is valued and respected. Administrators, faculty, and policy makers will find this discussion useful and meaningful.

Dr. Michael Miller has attempted a "giant stride" toward spawning the lucrativeness of participation in making decisions that impact the core of the education culture. The theme is not "centralization vs. decentralization" or "top-down or bottom-down" participation in the governance arena, but rather one of encouraging mental and philosophical competition to yield solutions to, and in some cases, archaic management and faculty disdainful attitude. There are no disguises, only attempts to discover the "real gold vein."

T. F. McCormack
Marion, Alabama

Section 1

Considering The Co-Governance Issue

Chapter 1
Conceptualizing Faculty Involvement in Governance
by Michael T. Miller

The collegiate environment has been defined and studied from a variety of perspectives. Whether examined by state legislative bodies or those interested in the success of college students, the issue of institutional management continuously arises as paramount to the future of the higher education enterprise. Recently, private sector leaders have called for institutions to be more like private sector businesses and less like governmental agencies. Accompanying their encouragement has been a series of calls to increase the empowerment of faculty (employees) in the governance process. Indeed, the movement to include employees in decision-making through such tools as TQM, CQI, or team-based work circles have spilled in to the higher education environment as never before.

The inclusion of faculty in the governance of higher education institutions dates to the earliest Colonial Colleges. Many of the early colleges in North America relied on faculty to handle the daily as well as general operations of the institutions. Although Baldridge (1982) argued that a truly ideal system of faculty involvement in governance has never existed, and Keller (1983) claimed that "presidents can't act and faculty won't" (p. 172), the potential benefits of shared governance, coupled with the movement for administrators to redefine their roles, places the involvement process at the forefront of issues facing higher education.

In a time of budgetary pressures driving policy development, the need to create an environment of campus-based consensus is vital to effective management (Bergmann, 1991). Gilmour (1991), in a national study of faculty governance, identified that 90% of all colleges and universities employ some form of formal governance units, such as faculty senates or faculty councils. The units typically employ either a representative or trustee based system of faculty involvement, and vary dramatically in terms of size and structure, ranging from all-inclusive town-hall type meetings for group decision-making to elections to present faculty to serve on a senate or council. These governance units typically make use of an elected leader and a slate of officers such as presidents, vice presidents, and committee chairs. The primary difference in the representative forms of governance includes trustee and delegate models. The trustee representative sees representation as a means of conveying issues and decisions to a select group of faculty, usually organized around an academic discipline. These faculty rely on grass-roots input to vote and make recommendations based on the collective will of the group. Conversely, the delegate form of representation holds that the faculty member acts in the good faith of the faculty. In such an instance, the specialization represented places faith and trust in the individual to act in their behalf.

Both types of governance foundations have been represented in collective bargaining situations for factors such as contract negotiations and delving as deep into academic matters as the identification or grading of journals in which to publish. Effective leadership requires both the knowledge of faculty cultures and leadership skills to coordinate and guide faculty efforts.

Leadership and Administration

The Chronicle of Higher Education Almanac (1996) reported that there are over 3,500 colleges and universities in the United States, of which approximately 2,164 are four-year institutions. Of those institutions, Gilmour (1991) identified that over 90% have some form of faculty governance body, whether it be a senate, forum, faculty or university council, or similar unit. This means that, on an annual basis, approximately 1,948 faculty members are being placed in positions of responsibility where they are seen as "first among equals" in representing faculty to administration. In this role, the leader of the faculty senate is placed in both a position of power and a position of jeopardy. The individual holds a tremendous degree of power in being charged with the responsibility of setting agendas, assigning committees, and establishing linkages with senior administrators within the institution. The faculty members are also placed in jeopardy by placing themselves in a vulnerable situation for the good of the faculty, a good which far exceeds the rewards to the individual faculty member. Trow (1990) ironically noted that this faculty leader position, typically a president or chair of a faculty senate or forum, does not result in or serve as a transitory position for a faculty member to move into an administrative position. Conversely, Westerfield (1997) has identified that service, university-wide or in some instances college-wide, provides experience in decision-making and exposure to the different academic and nonacademic actors which comprise the collegiate environment. Utilizing such a rationale, leadership in a faculty senate actually can be seen as a means to position an individual for a future of administrative responsibility, despite Trow's contention that faculty members holding the leadership position actually feel animosity or anger toward administration and do not want to become involved in such a situation.

The National Data Base on Faculty Involvement in Governance (NDBFIG) in 1996 and 1997 focused their activities on a series of studies of the faculty governance leader. In a presentation to the Eastern Educational Research Association (Miller, 1997A), the leaders of faculty senates were identified as predominantly associate or full professors, were from the liberal arts, with some representation from the sciences and education, and two-thirds of them were male. The report further noted that these faculty leaders saw their primary role as providing a sense of direction for the faculty senate. In such an instance, Miller claimed, the faculty senate president establishes the pace and climate for the governance unit as being one of either action, or conversely, one of passivity in dealing with administration. Miller also identified the tasks of developing networks and linkages, taking care of the details of the senate, developing a sense of pride in senate activities, obtaining and allocating resources, and developing data bases as the key tasks of presiding over a senate. Ironically, faculty senates when viewed as a legislative body, or as a body which provides a series of checks and balances to an administration and board of directors, must rely heavily on institutional research activities to consider such issues as, for example, grade inflation, merit pay, parking decals, costs structures, tuition pricing, etc. If such is true, then the idea of developing data bases as a role of the faculty senate president seems odd to be at the bottom of the list of tasks.

Miller also reported that the motivations for serving as the chair of a faculty senate or similar governance unit were primarily based on having a sense of empowerment, fulfilling a sense of responsibility, or the sense of importance associated with the decision-making. These motivations were followed closely by the motivator that the leader was asked to serve or to fulfill a sense of professionalism. Incidentally, some faculty senates reported that they actually have difficulty in finding slates of officers to run for executive or leadership positions of prominence in their governance units. Not to claim that their worth is not great, but rather, the commitment of time, energy, ingenuity and perhaps the issue of jeopardy all come into play for the faculty representative.

NDBFIG research projects concluded with the examination of skills needed for leading a faculty senate. In the case of the national study of 100 faculty senate presidents, survey respondents (i.e. presidents or chairs) agreed most that they must have strong skills in judgment, oral communication, organizational ability, written communication skills, leadership skills, a strong value structure, stress tolerance, and problem analysis skills. The study results indicated no significant differences based on types of institutions involved, and few differences between those leaders who saw themselves as being process oriented as compared to those who saw themselves as being task oriented.

As Trow (1990) alluded, the faculty governance unit leader can be somewhat removed and suspicious of administrators, an issue embedded within the writings of many others. These are issues of jurisdiction and span of control. Span-of-control issues, while regulated largely through legal discussions, give way to the jurisdiction of whether the governance unit serves as either a policy-making or policy-implementing unit, or rather, a power balancing unit of the administration. Although the provost or vice president of academic affairs position may typically be seen as one of advocating faculty rights and responsibilities, the faculty senate or governance unit has begun to be seen as the primary facilitator of faculty rights. This question of jurisdiction gives way to the topical considerations brought forward on an annual basis. Utilizing stringent legal interpretations, faculty have few rights in areas of curricular matter. However, faculty members are continually placed in positions of responsibility outside of questions of academic matter. For example, faculty are typically called upon to help develop and create policy on merit pay, admissions requirements, scholarship distribution, and facility use and regulation.

The question of jurisdiction can also be considered from the framework of the responsibility of the academic unit, e.g., college or school, as compared to that of the institution as a whole. Although most institutions will make use of one faculty governance body, e.g., the senate or council, some institutions will also employ collective governing bodies at the college or school level. Miller (1997B) identified one such case at The University of Alabama where the College of Education operated a Faculty Forum in addition to a university wide faculty senate. In such a circumstance, the complexity of delineating unit and institution-wide responsibilities can become tenuous. For example, on issues concerning undergraduate core curriculum, the matter of syllabus or course approval must flow from administrative offices to the governance unit, while simultaneously flowing to both decision-making bodies. Similarly, institutional merit money may be distributed differently from college to college, where a unit-wide senate or governing body may be better prepared to address issues facing the particular college or school as compared to an all-inclusive faculty senate.

Modeling Involvement

Questions of jurisdiction over faculty rights, responsibilities, and privileges have led to numerous conceptual models of how it is that faculty members are involved, to what extent they are involved, and what their role is in that involvement. Questions of jurisdiction have also been examined and debated in light of institutional effectiveness (Boyd, 1985). Some of these questions and models have been faculty based, while others are administrative or decision-making process based.

One of the most popular models has been Birnbaum's (1988) depiction of higher education institutions being classified as a combination of four different institutional typologies, including collegial, political, anarchical, and bureaucratic, resulting in what he termed a "cybernetic" institution. In such a setting, he argued, decisions are made through a combination of power struggles, formal office-based power, and the distribution of power for the sake of decision making and insulation from accountability variables. Although this has been a widely received framework for examining institutional decision making, several models have also arisen which are directly linked to the involvement of faculty in governance.

Legislative Model

One of the more recent conceptual models for the involvement of faculty in governance to be formalized in literature has been the conceptualization of a faculty governance unit as serving as a form of legislative branch which must work to hold in check the activities of an executive branch, on a college campus comprised of administrators and administrative units (Figure 1).

Figure 1

The Academic Senate in Higher Education

Legislative Branch	Executive Branch	Judicial Branch
Faculty	Administrators	Trustees
(all ranks)	(directors, chairs, deans, vice presidents, presidents)	(governing boards and to some extent advisory councils of business and industry leaders or alumni)

The relationship between these two "branches" is then held in check or balanced with what could be considered a judicial branch, that is, the board of directors, governors, or trustees who lay the parameters for the involvement of faculty in different decision-making issues. The board also determines who has the right to do what, what policy can legally be implemented, and finalizes decisions related to the institution, etc. On a somewhat responsive basis, a constituent body must bring the issue before the judicial body prior to its taking action. As such, the board serves much like a court where legal action must be taken on legislation passed by Congress. Also within this framework is the concept that institutional administrators from the dean or director level through the campus chief academic or chief executive officer will influence the behaviors and actions of those serving in a legislative body. For example, deans, vice presidents, provosts, and presidents encourage faculty to embrace something such as research productivity. Nonacademic matters may vary broadly, including an issue of parking policy or whether the administration believes that a campus should be entirely pedestrian. If such a movement comes from the faculty, then the administration is much better situated to act on the matter, develop, and implement the policy to that effect. In so doing, there then arises real questions of ethical power uses by senior administrators, particularly in working with untenured faculty or in working with faculty on the creation of post-tenure review programs. Although this model has not been validated, it does represent a visualization of a campus community driven largely by the competition for scarce resources and political and partisan behavior.

The concept of shared governance, similar to the federal system of the branches of government, is predicated on the belief that individuals want to be involved, and that they will be honest, truthful, and sincere in their dealings. The result in this type of conceptualization is the development and joint reliance on coalition development among faculty subgroups, and the "lobbying" by administrators for faculty support of decision-making and policy formation.

Watch-Dog Model

Clark Kerr (1991) contended that faculty members gained the potential to greatly enhance their collective voice in decision making during the turbulence following the academic freedom movement of the late 1960s. He also held that faculty members have largely been reluctant to take advantage of this ability, noting that many faculty have become passive in demanding rights and responsibilities in decision making.

The responsibility of holding administrators accountable to faculty and students alike has resulted in the resurgence of a watchdog model of faculty involvement. In this scenario, a small, select, and highly motivated group of faculty work to stay informed of administrative behaviors, and alert other faculty and campus based groups of decisions which may negatively effect the perceived "good" of the campus. This small group of faculty may operate independent of formal senates or councils, and has been informally referred to as 'faculty radicals.'

These 'radicals' often find a sense of fulfillment and motivation in their belief that they maintain the integrity and best interests of the campus community. Additionally, the common belief has been that large numbers of faculty prove ineffective in keeping a close watch on administrators, but large groups are believed to be essential in times of crises to maintain some degree of faculty control over administrators.

Ladder Approach

Faculty involvement, as seen through both the perspective of faculty and administrators, has been classified as a process which allows for the empowerment of faculty members. This empowerment, which can be equated with span of control and responsibility issues, has been conceptualized along the framework of Arnstein's (1976) and Murphy's (1991) work, depicted as a ladder of involvement. Within this model, faculty members are involved to varying degrees based on administrative allowances, where individual administrators and administrative units work through policy and behavior to involve or restrict the involvement of faculty in a host of decision-making episodes.

Arnstein developed a ladder of citizen involvement based on the contention that citizens, namely parents, have a right and responsibility to be involved in local secondary school decision-making. Drawing on much of the literature and practical involvement of site-based management and citizen responsibility, Arnstein contended that parents and citizens are involved to varying extents, dependent upon the willingness of the local school authority to allow for shared authority.

Arnstein's work was applied to the context of faculty involvement, adapting the "ladder" to reflect the position and environment of higher education (Miller, McCormack, Maddox, & Seagren, 1996). This conceptualization holds that faculty can be entirely restricted (Non-Involvement) in their involvement, resulting in feelings of manipulation (see Figure 2).

Figure 2

Ladder of Faculty Involvement in Governance

8	Faculty Control	
7	Delegated Power	Degrees of Faculty Power
6	Partnership	
5	Placation	
4	Consultation	Degrees of Tokenism
3	Informing	
2	Therapy	Non-Participation
1	Manipulation	

As administrators allow for increased involvement, faculty feelings of ownership may be fluid and flow through levels of therapy, information sharing, and placation. In such a situation, senior administrators may involve faculty to the extent that data and decisions are presented as a matter of information, and may allow for restricted involvement to placate faculty needs in feeling ownership or responsibility for the institution or academic unit.

The characteristics typically identified within each level of involvement tend to have a primarily administrative focus, as indicated by span of control and delegation, in the lower levels of Manipulation (Level 1) and Therapy (Level 2). Higher levels of involvement tend to be more faculty-centered, and offer faculty members the ability to make decisions and function within the collegiate environment. Munn (1996), based on an extensive literature review, defined the characteristics of each level from the standpoint of both administrators and faculty, and concluded that the governance process in higher education is based entirely on the human relations aspects and interpersonal skills of administrators and the faculty who participate in the institution (see Figure 3, pp. 14-19).

Figure 3

Administrator and Faculty Roles in Progressive Involvement

Ladder Rung	Administrators	Faculty
Level 1: **Manipulation** Faculty involvement or lack of involvement may result in manipulation by decision-making administrators.	Responsible to their institutions. See the institution as comparable to private sector firms. Suggest ideas of "top down" management. Coercive power; feel they have the ability to punish if faculty does not accept their attempts at influence. Separate jurisdiction because of specialization. More likely to believe that certain academic decisions do not require faculty involvement. Identified with 'red tape,' constraints, and outside pressures that seek to alter the institution.	Loss of faculty control is related to increased size and complexity and the division of faculty into different departments, committees, and other units. Expert power; faculty accepts influence from administrators. Excluded from faculty senates or councils creating feelings of alienation and resentment. Faculty must insist on rights and responsibilities in appropriate governance roles (such as curriculum, graduation requirements, etc.).

Figure 3
(cont.)
Administrator and Faculty Roles in Progressive Involvement

Ladder Rung	Administrators	Faculty
Level 1: **Manipulation** (continued)	Fund raising and externally focused activities; funding priorities turned into goals. Networking based among similar professionals. A sense of powerlessness that comes from one's own limited ability to exert influence upward.	
Level 2: **Therapy** The degree of non-participation by faculty can also be used as a therapeutic endeavor for both faculty release of responsibility and administrative control.	By decision-making, administrators take responsibility and administrative control. State executives or legislative agencies become involved in program reviews, administrative operations, budgeting and planning, causing administrative chaos and confusion. Reward power; ability to offer rewards and remove or decrease negative influences. Speak with a single voice to powerful external agencies.	Seen by administrators as self-interested, unconcerned with controlling costs or unwilling to respond to legitimate requests for accountability. Seeks affiliation goals; "we're in this together." A way to get to know others, as it looks good to those in power.

Figure 3
(cont.)
Administrator and Faculty Roles in Progressive Involvement

Ladder Rung	Administrators	Faculty
Level 2: **Therapy** (continued)	Should provide for joint conducive environment committees participation in governance. Ensure due process rights of all parties (students, faculty, and staff). Build strong business and industry partnerships. Emphasis on long-range planning and the mandated search for external funding.	Faculty should work harder to cooperate with administration.
Levels 3, 4, & 5: **Informing, Placation, and Consultation**	Create policy and provide visionary leadership. Generally more conservative in attitudes than faculty. Subject to external control and funding agencies that bypass and weaken institutional administration. Should educate and encourage faculty involvement.	Responsible to themselves and their peers and their primary discipline. Responsible for academic personnel matters; assessing the qualifications of colleagues. Curriculum affects the faculty as much as the faculty influence the curriculum.

Figure 3
(cont.)
Administrator and Faculty Roles in Progressive Involvement

Ladder Rung	Administrators	Faculty
Levels 3, 4, & 5: **Informing, Placation, and Consultation** (continued)	Should increase communication with faculty and lead by example.	Funded research based primarily on the activities of individual faculty. Often consulted on a technical level. Participate in institutional activities. Provide community service; trying to make things better for the good of the university and students. Convince administration that the faculty voice is valuable in the decision-making process on non-academic management issues such as budget and planning. Faculty senate is utilized as a conduit through which faculty participation is solicited. Neutral "consultants" are utilized to mediate faculty-administration dealings.

Figure 3
(cont.)
Administrator and Faculty Roles in Progressive Involvement

Ladder Rung	Administrators	Faculty
Levels 6, 7, & 8: **Partnership, Delegated Power, and Faculty Control**	Not to govern scholars but rather to serve as their assistants. Have lesser understanding and support of principles of academic freedom. Have an acceptance of hierarchical authority. Set organizational goals and maintain standards of performance. Implement procedures that will pass judicial tests of equitable treatment. Effectiveness equals administration and faculty with shared expertise.	Obtains influence by developing strong sense of professionalism and by asserting and protecting academic values. Must agree to a common code. Requirements to rationalize budget formats. Through senate, council, forum, or other body, faculty create resolution and provide the substance for effective operation of the institution. Responsible for curriculum, instruction, faculty status, rank, and the academic aspects of student life. Serve as the academic focus for teaching. Responsible for faculty recruitment and promotion.

**Figure 3
(cont.)
Administrator and Faculty Roles in Progressive Involvement**

Ladder Rung	Administrators	Faculty
Levels 6, 7, & 8: **Partnership, Delegated Power, and Faculty Control** (continued)		Produce, apply, preserve and communicate knowledge.
		Reduce culture of fear for non-tenured faculty.
		Must allow time for involvement in governance.
		Responsible for education of students through teaching and research.
		Faculty members lend a 'certain credibility' to donors in fund raising.
		Faculty are interested in having access to decision makers and the opportunity for input.
		Communication is a necessity between faculty senate and academic administration.
		Faculty are empowered to question policy through a well-articulated process.

Six Perceptions Model

A team of researchers at the University of Washington conducted an in-depth study of how faculty perceived their role in the governance process and the activities they undertook to be involved or non-involved (Williams, Gore, Broches, & Lostoski, 1987). By developing a set a statements to be clustered by faculty members, the research team identified six categories by which faculty chose to be identified These categories (collegials, activists, acceptors, hierarchicals, copers, and disengaged) were then presented in a schematic of the governance process, where they were further defined by variables of concern for governance issues, confidence in the faculty's governance role, and age (see Figure 4).

Figure 4

Six Perceptions of Governance Model

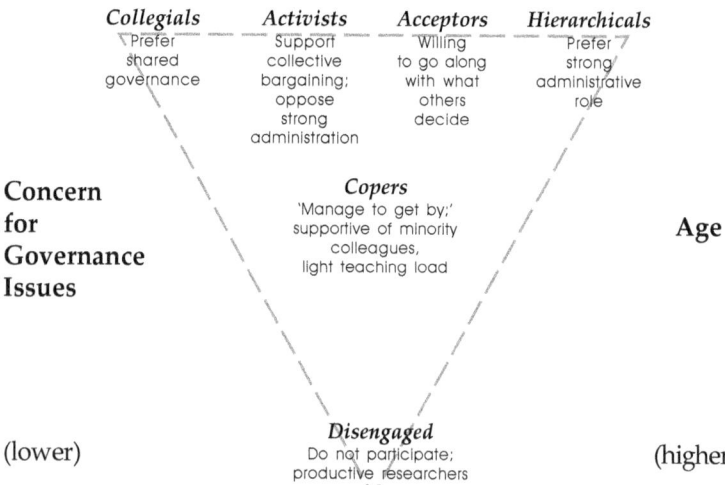

This model takes the form of an inverted pyramid, with faculty categorizations situated according to their different perceptions of the governance process, perceptions which often dictate or reflect the willingness of individuals to become involved. The categories presented are:

Collegial: Prefer shared governance approach.
Oppose collective bargaining.
Oppose strong administrative role.
Tenured. 2/3 are full professors.

Activists: Supportive of collective bargaining and other mechanisms for increasing the faculty's governance role, which they view presently as weak.
Reject strong administrative role.
More approving of traditional collegial mechanisms than Acceptors.

Acceptors: More accepting of faculty's governance role than the Hierarchicals.
Willing to go along with what the others decide.
Limited experience in Faculty Senate.
Less concerned than the Copers for women/minority faculty.

Hierarchicals: Prefer strong administrative role.
Respond negatively to strong faculty role and to collegial mechanisms now in place.
Reject collective bargaining.

Copers: Middle-range faculty who are managing to "get by."
Many associate professors.
Light teaching load.
Supportive of minority/women faculty colleagues.
More supportive of collective bargaining than the Disengaged.

Disengaged: Do not participate in faculty government.
Tend to disparage faculty governance role.
Oppose collective bargaining.
Productive researchers.
(Williams, Gore, Broches, & Lostoski, 1987, p. 648)

The authors reaffirmed their notation that governance activities can be classified along traditional lines, such as those presented by Birnbaum, yet the process can be more fluid and situational forcing the blurring of these lines. As such, the model draws strength from the contention that faculty involvement is based primarily on how specific issues or topics touch on personal value systems. The response of faculty, then, can be reflective of coalition building and the position or support of administration and fellow colleagues.

The Research and Teaching Paradox

Many colleges and universities express concern over the extent to which their faculty engage in teaching and research activities. Although service is certainly valued, institutional scope and mission typically dictate primary faculty attention to either excellence in the classroom or excellence in the advancement and creation of knowledge. These two roles are not dichotomous, but have been repeatedly identified as barriers to involving faculty in governance activities. The employing institution identifies the primary emphasis for faculty expectation not through letters of appointment (see Appendix 1 for sample letter), but rather through a process of informal pressure to perform, merit pay, promotion, and tenure.

Scholars and practitioners alike have argued strongly that there is a possibility for a peaceful coexistence between teaching activities and research, however, a primary difficulty reported by new faculty are the divergent paths these two expectations often take (Jungnickel, 1990). The context of this coexistence lies in the ability to extend research into the classroom, while simultaneously viewing research as a form of teaching. Additionally, teaching can be viewed as a form of scholarship, allowing for constant renewal of academic matters and continuous evaluation and assessment of student learning. Regardless of the vantage point for the teaching and research debate, the issue of service has traditionally been minimized at best.

The concept of institutional service maintains that faculty members have a responsibility to be involved in the successful operation of the institution (Birnbaum, 1991). In addition to the formal faculty senate or governance unit, most institutions make use of a comprehensive system and structure of committees. Comprehensive, research-oriented universities will typically employ over a hundred such committees, ranging in responsibility from facilities, athletics, student judicial matters, and institutional research to international students, student media, orientation, alumni relations, and calendar planning (see Appendix 2 for a typical listing of institutional committees). These committees often allow for faculty to identify their areas of primary interest, yet may occasionally still find difficulty in garnering faculty attendance and participation.

The divergent orientations of faculty have been the subject of research conducted by the NDBFIG project during 1994 and 1996. Exploring faculty who work in research-oriented colleges and universities and those who work at primarily teaching-oriented colleges and universities, this research has suggested a strong degree of similarity in their perceptions of both an ideal governance process and the role faculty should have in institutional governance (Miller, McCormack, Maddox, & Seagren, 1996).

Despite these similarities, faculty continue to proclaim difficulty in finding the time, energy, and creative resources necessary to effectively participate in governance through either committee work or formal governance structures. Miller (1997B) identified this level of involvement by faculty in governance as so distressing that in one institution the overall attendance rate of faculty at governance unit meetings was 47% for all faculty, with full-professors and assistant professors having the lowest attendance rates at 43% and 53% respectively, and associate professors having the highest attendance rate at 65%.

Legal Parameters of Involvement

College faculty members are typically employed without a formal written contract, and yet the tendering of an oral contract by the employing institution can be equally as formidable in the courtroom (Miles, 1987). Rather than formal contracts at four-year universities, most institutions make use of a letter of appointment (see Sample in Appendix A) which identifies the salary, position, title, and general responsibilities. Regardless of institutional typology, most faculty are expected to teach, engage in some form of service, whether to the institution or to a professional association, and in many cases, conduct academic research. This tri-fold expectation can be further refined within individual institution merit systems, which, for example, will reward excellence in the classroom, or conversely, excellence in research and publication. Both of these areas, teaching and research, have subsequently received considerable attention in scholarly and practitioner-oriented literature and professional development activities.

The least attention by scholars and practitioners has been devoted to the expectation of providing what is loosely termed "service." The service component of an academic appointment provides both the opportunity to help in shaping the form of the academic unit or institution, and forum for developing a peer support system which may prove to be valuable during tenure and promotion activities. The concept of service, also discussed as academic citizenship, often requires individual faculty members to engage in activities related to the governance of an institution. Although identified as crucial to institutional effectiveness and professional survival, many junior faculty are discouraged from involvement in service based on the contention that such an activity takes too much valuable time away from teaching and scholarship.

Although expected and seldom rewarded, the involvement of faculty in institutionally-related service has limited, at best, legal precedence. In *Harry Connick v. Sheila Myers*, the U. S. Supreme Court found that public employees do not have a right to criticize their employers under the protection of the First Amendment. The case concerned Myers' behavior in the District Attorney's Office of New Orleans, where she criticized her employer, Connick, for transferring her to an alternate office and his personal behavior. She prepared and circulated a questionnaire and made statements about Connick's behavior and effect on the workplace. The opinion of the Court, as rendered by Justice White, noted that comments by a public employee outside of those made for the public good can be cause for termination, and that public employees do not have a right to criticize their employer. The Court further noted that

> Ordinary dismissals from government service which violate no fixed tenure or applicable statute or regulation are not subject to judicial review even if reasons for dismissal are alleged to be mistaken or unreasonable. (*Connick v. Myers*, 1983, p. 1684)

Another legal precedent which restricted the involvement of faculty in decision-making external to academic matters has been *Minnesota State Board for Community Colleges v. Knight, et al.* In this matter, addressed in the U. S. Supreme Court in 1983-1984, the community college faculty in Minnesota challenged the constitutionality of the Minnesota Public Employment Labor Relations Act which held that administrators must engage in official exchanges of views with faculty through exclusive association representation. The Supreme Court held that "faculty members do not have a constitutional right to participate in policy making in academic institution" (*U. S. Supreme Court Reports* 79 L Ed 2d, p. 302). In delivering the opinion of the Court, Justice O'Connor noted that the State policy was one that encouraged professional interaction through 'meet and confer' sessions, and found that the representation from the faculty association also served as the representation for 'meet and confer' opportunities. Further noted was that public employees, e.g. the faculty, have no legal basis for having a right to 'meet and confer' with administrators.

A further assertion by the Courts concerning the level of authority granted to faculty members came in the 1983 case of *Ballard v. Blount*. The U.S. District Court for the Northern District of Georgia denied a salary raise to a college instructor, a denial based primarily on the instructor's criticism of the institution's academic policy. The Court held that the faculty member's criticism of institutional policy was not a matter of public concern, and thus was not protected by first amendment rights. Further, the *Harleston v. Jeffries* decision in 1994 provided an extension of the regulation of faculty academic freedom demonstrated through public speech.

As a result of these court decisions, administrative bodies have no legal right to request the involvement of faculty in matters such as budgetary allocations, facilities, athletic regulations, and student affairs administration. Compounding this legal consideration, many faculty request or require some form of compensation, such as credit toward merit pay or tenure and promotion for involvement. A national union has similarly noted that compensation may be a necessity for taking on additional work-related responsibilities (Kameras, 1996), yet all typically agree that consensus development in the workplace is important.

The entire concept of sharing authority is based on the contention that an institution can operate more efficiently and more effectively by involving various stakeholders in institutional operations (McCormack, 1995). The result, while often positive, naturally lends itself to informal structures and processes which simultaneously enhance and detract from institutional effectiveness. The intent of this chapter was to provide a basic framework for further discussion of shared authority in various areas of concern. Indeed, the framework suggested that position responsibilities identified and the formal legal parameters presented on faculty and administrators alike provide strength to the issue of exploring the political and dynamic world of faculty involvement in governance.

For Discussion

1. What are the cultural criteria for situating a framework for shared authority at different types of institutions? How can these frameworks be identified and tailored to institutionally specific factors?
2. What institutional factors influence the behaviors undertaken by a faculty governance unit leader? What resultant training needs and areas of skill mastery can be identified?
3. How is attention to teaching, research, and service at your institution promoted, encouraged, and rewarded? What specific actions or episodes continue this reward structure, and how is this reward structure aligned with academic units and institutional mission statements and visions?
4. How do informal institutional characteristics work to define administrative jurisdiction, and how does this affect the issue of span of control for faculty, administrators, and trustees?
5. What rewards are offered to your faculty for being involved in shared authority activities? Aside from external rewards for involvement, what internal rewards can be linked to faculty involvement?
6. What are the legal parameters typically placed on a governance process? How are these defined with faculty, and to what extent do these decisions inhibit or enhance governance behaviors?
7. Is the involvement of faculty in the governance process

monitored and evaluated? If so, what measures can be devised to assure an effective participation in governance?

Chapter 2
Benefits and Barriers to Shared Authority
by Jennifer P. Evans

The popular practices of participative management, total quality management, and site-based management are similar in their intent to involve employees in the decision-making process. What these approaches to managing employees and work processes share is an acknowledgment that people need to be involved in the critical decisions that affect their lives. Modern organizational theorists agree that when employees have a lack of control over important work-related events they feel alienated from their jobs and the organization. Alienation is a state of powerlessness experienced by workers in companies and institutions when they are unable to satisfy self-realization and ego-esteem needs (Kanungo, 1992). The alienated employee has no sense of freedom and control within the organization. Consequently, both the individual workers and the organization suffer.

The anecdote for the alienated employee is increased autonomy and control over one's behaviors and work environment (Argyris, 1964). This self-determination results in empowerment. Empowerment is a management practice which enables employees to participate in the decisions related to task accomplishment, creating a heightened sense of personal efficacy. As a result, both the individual workers and the organization benefit.

Those who study how work is accomplished in organizations agree that success partly depends upon the development of employees and their ability to communicate effectively. A dialectic perspective of employee development reveals how the struggle of an adult's need for autonomy and self-growth conflicts with the organization's need to control how work is accomplished by employees. A dialectic perspective of effective communication reveals how the struggle of a adult's need to interact horizontally and vertically as a means of communicating ideas and solutions to improve the work flow conflicts with the organization's need to define levels of employee involvement and thus limit the potential of effective (purposeful) employee communication.

The development of employees and their ability to communicate effectively is mediated by their level of involvement in the decision-making processes that affect their jobs. Figure 5 depicts the interaction of worker alienation and empowerment.

Figure 5

Interaction of Worker Alienation and Empowerment

Minimum Employment Input Management makes decisions	Maximum Employment Input Employee makes decisions
<u>Alienated Workers</u>	<u>Empowered Workers</u>
Communicate only with supervisor and coworkers	Communicate with employees at all levels and areas

The purpose of this chapter is to examine the benefits reaped by involved faculty and the barriers that often prevent or discourage faculty participation. These issues are presented within the context of organizational communication, business, and higher education. The terms "employee" and "manager" are interchangeable with the terms "faculty" and "administration" throughout the chapter.

The examination begins with an overview of decision-making and an historical perspective of employee involvement in organizations. The positive outcomes of shared decision-making are presented, along with the issues that stifle and often prevent involvement. A view of current studies of higher education faculty leads to practical suggestions and recommendations for employee involvement and a case study for applying these strategies.

Current State of Decision-Making

Three factors contribute to a group's ability to make decisions: group process and communication, group leadership, and organizational influences.

Group Process and Communication

The Decision-Making Process: Researchers of individual, group, and organizational decision making conclude that people experience a predictable structure or pattern during the decision-making process, typically including three phases: 1) Orientation, 2) Conflict, and 3) Acceptance. This pattern is generalized from the Phase Theorems which suggest that any group involved in the decision-making process will experience at least these general phases of growth (Bales & Strodtbeck, 1951; Bennis & Shepard, 1956).

During the first stage of decision-making, termed 'orientation,' group members socialize and orient themselves with the task. Members begin to organize themselves. The second stage is known as conflict among members. Researchers recognize conflict as a natural process that is a prerequisite for the development of individual members into a cohesive and mature team. Conflict is followed by acceptance of the group decision(s). At the very least, all groups experience the phases of orientation, conflict, and acceptance; however, studies of group decision-making reveal that the decision-making process is unique for groups and is a complex process that does not "fit" into one neat, general structure.

Communication: During the early stages of the structural development process, the members' interpersonal communication styles are critical to the development and growth of the group. Members who communicate with a passive style of communication, which is characterized by being friendly, attentive, relaxed, and precise, demonstrate a willingness to consider the ideas and feelings of others (Norton, 1978; 1983). This interpersonal style of being other-oriented encourages participants to be forthright in their conversations and sets a tone of trust and openness.

Members who communicate with an active style of communication, which is characterized by being dramatic, dominant, animated, and sometimes argumentative, demonstrate an inward tendency (Norton, 1978; 1983). In other words, an active communicator is self-oriented and does not demonstrate concern for the listener. This style of communicating hinders the opportunity for group members to "open-up" and share ideas.

Open communication is characterized by people being willing to share personal information with others in hopes of reciprocity and intimacy (Norton, 1978; 1983). In a work setting, open communication is essential for the development of trusting relationships. In fact, being open with others is the most critical step in earning the trust of coworkers. Both active and passive styles may include characteristics of open communicators.

Experts recommend a realistic approach to communicating which involves recognizing one's natural style and balancing it with other interpersonal approaches. Groups continuously evolve and change over time. As described in phase theory, individuals constantly pattern and restructure their groups according to their interpretations of interpersonal norms, rules of socialization, and the perceived availability of resources. New members, such as faculty, are initiated into the norms of the group and introduce fresh resources, status, and social norms. Communication, at the interpersonal and group level, is a critical attribute for the development of members into a cohesive body of decision makers.

Group Leadership

Another factor affecting the group's ability to make a decision is the group leader. What type of leadership style does this person implement in a group environment? Is the individual a team player or an autocrat? Does the leader place importance on relationships or tasks? Was the person selected, elected, or appointed to the position of group leader? To what extent were the group members involved in this process?

The characteristics and style of the group leader greatly influence the tone and climate of the group. Vroom and Yetton (1973) have identified five decision procedures which are typically used for decisions involving multiple subordinates. The fifth procedure, Joint Decision Making, is appropriate for democratic-style committees in which members participate as equals and a consensus is desired. The five procedures are:

Autocratic I:
   The leader solves the problem using only available information.

Autocratic II:
   The leader makes the decision after obtaining necessary information from subordinates. The leader may or may not share the problem with employees.

Consultative I:
   The leader shares the problem with relevant subordinates individually. The employees provide ideas and suggestions, but do not meet as a group. The leader makes the decision which may or may not reflect employee input.

Consultative II:
   The leader shares the problem with employees as a group and asks for their suggestions and ideas. The leader makes the decision which may or may not reflect employee input.

Joint Decision Making:
   The leader shares the problem with the group. All members, including the leader, generate and evaluate alterna-

tives. Group members attempt to reach an agreement (consensus) which is accepted by the leader. The group leader functions as a chair person and agrees to adopt the group's decision.

Probably the most essential characteristic of a group leader is flexibility. The key for leaders is to recognize which style they gravitate towards and make appropriate adjustments. In a higher education environment which encourages open communication and freedom of expression, the joint decision-making approach is optimal.

Organizational Influences

The third key factor in determining a group's ability to make decisions is its limitations from external entities such as organizational influences or regulations. Is the group's decision subject to a veto by a higher authority? For example, a faculty committee decision may be supported by the committee chair, yet vetoed by the chair, area head or dean. Do organizational rules, such as travel restrictions or budget constraints, prevent the implementation of decisions? Are group members required to make a decision within specific guidelines that actually prevent the remedy of the situation? For instance, the dean of a college of education has appointed a faculty committee to improve the process of reviewing applications for graduate programs. However, the graduate school dean has just revised the university-wide guidelines for graduate admissions and has deemed them nonnegotiable. The committee members find themselves in a lose-lose situation in which they cannot implement decisions to improve the admissions process.

One type of organizational influence, which may also be described as an external influence, involves issues that are regulated by governmental, legal, or accrediting bodies, such as the Equal Employment Opportunity Commission (EEOC), Occupational Safety and Hazard Association (OSHA), and state agencies governing teacher preparation or national and state accrediting bodies. It is incumbent upon decision makers to be aware of these regulations and to seek expert guidance in interpreting them in order to resolve issues within the legal boundaries of the institution.

A group decision that is reached using a truly democratic process in which all members have equal power is possible, depending upon the maturity of the group, the role of the group leader, and the willingness of external constituents to accept the decision.

Key to Success

Group process and communication, group leadership, and organizational factors contribute to the success of the group decision-making process. Other factors, such as stakeholders, time, and information, are just as critical to the decision process. Following are samples of additional factors to consider:

Stakeholders are any individuals who have power because:
— they are responsible for the final decision;
— they are in a position to implement the decision or prevent it from being implemented;
— they are likely to be affected by the outcome of the decision;
— they are considered to be experts or have critical information relative to the decision or the decision-making process.

There is no right way to make a decision. Making the best decision depends upon:

Stakeholder buy-in: How much do they need to be involved so that they can confidently support implementation of the process?

Time available: How much time can be spent on decision-making?

Importance: How important or inconsequential is the issue to people in the organization?

Information needed: Who has the information or expertise that can contribute to making a quality decision?

Capability: How capable and experienced are people in operating as decision makers or as a decision-making team?

Building teamwork: What is the potential value of using this opportunity to create a stronger team?

Amount and accuracy of information: Do we have all the information we need? Is it accurate?

Quality of thinking: Are members informed and participating in discourse?

Importance of group communication: Group discussion allows members to distribute and pool information resources, catch and remedy errors of judgment, and have a means of intragroup persuasion.

The Struggle with Authentic and Inauthentic Employee Involvement

For several decades, leaders of organizations have struggled to find the perfect balance or level of employee involvement for their workers. This struggle, which is clearly documented in business, communication, psychology, and education literature, began with the intent of making employees feel good about their work. As management theories evolved, so did the concept that authentic employee participation is an essential ingredient for individual and organizational success.

Historical Perspective

The Classical Approach. Human resource development can be viewed as an evolution of how individuals who work within an organizational setting are viewed by those who manage them. Modern theories of organization were developed during the Industrial Revolution and were perceived as theories of management because they reflected the interest of managers and were implemented by managers to improve productivity. The theories emerging from the Industrial Revolution, referred to as the classical ap-

proach, were models that resembled efficient machines.
The "father" of scientific management, Frederick Winslow Taylor, is considered the first management theorist. Taylor's (1967) theory of Scientific Management represented a classical autocratic philosophy of management in which employees were hired to carry out prespecified duties as directed by management. Taylor's (1967) *The Principles of Scientific Management* is considered by many to be the seminal work on organizational and decision theory. In this work, Taylor wrote "the principle objective of management should be to secure the maximum prosperity for the employer, coupled with the maximum prosperity for each employee" (p. 9). Taylor defined maximum prosperity for the employee as "the development of each man to his state of maximum efficiency" (p. 9).

Taylor's theory was characterized by clearly defined rules, laws, and a separation of management and workers. Communication in this model was viewed only as a tool for using orders and gaining worker compliance (Kreps, 1990). For example, an excerpt about functional management from Taylor's book *Shop Management* (1911) reveals his notion of organizational communication and employee involvement:

> Certainly the most marked outward characteristic of functional management lies in the fact that each workman, instead of coming in direct contact with the management at one point only, namely, through his gang boss, receives his daily orders and help directly from eight different bosses, each of whom performs his own particular function. Four of these bosses are in the planning room and three of these send their orders to and receive their returns from the men, usually in writing. (p. 99)

The predominant theme of the classical approach, as introduced by Taylor and developed by others such as Max Weber (1947), was that its theorists discounted all human factors in their quest to organize work.

Human Relations and Human Resources. After the traditional (classical) approach to management was established, leadership studies in the early Twentieth Century explored managerial approaches to employee participation within organizations. These studies found that two distinct theories, human relations and human resources, pervaded their view of subordinates (Miles, 1965).

Focusing on the role of the individual in the organization was the theme of human relations theorists who recognized the limitations of classical theory. Human relations theory posited that increased involvement by the worker would lead to increased productivity. The human relations theory, which was influenced by Herbert Blumer's (1969) work in symbolic interactionism, is a perspective in social psychology for understanding the nature of social interaction. Two major extensions of research on human relations were Herzberg's (1966) theory of motivation and Fiedler's (1964) contingency theory. These leadership theories were founded on the human relations notion that supportive leader communication positively affects productivity and morale (Kreps, 1990).

The key element in the human relations approach to managing employees, according to Miles (1965), was the objective of making organization members feel useful and important to the overall effort. Thus, although employees were asked to offer suggestions and opinions, their input was often not taken seriously by management. Although the human relations approach acknowledged the importance of the individual within the organization, it shared with the traditional approach the ultimate goal of worker compliance with managerial authority.

The human resources approach to understanding organizational life stemmed from researchers who were disenchanted with the cosmetic applications of human relations theory. The approach offered a more enlightened strategy for meeting the needs of organization members and increasing their participation in organizational activities (Miles, 1965). A key point of departure from previous theories is that human resources valued the role of upward communications and was concerned with the total organizational climate. Leadership theories, such as McGregor's theory X and theory Y, and Maslow's hierarchy of needs, grew out of the human resources theory (Kreps, 1990).

Managers who embraced this philosophy deemed it their duty to unlock the creative potential of their employees so that each individual contributed maximum effort in decision-making activities. Instead of making employees feel useful, the human resources model suggested that when individuals are involved in making decisions that impact the organization, the organization is more productive and employee satisfaction levels are higher as a result of making significant contributions to organizational success (Miles, 1965).

Figure 6

Interaction of Worker Alienation and Empowerment

Classical/Traditional Management Style	Human Relations Management Style
Minimum employee input Management makes decisions ↓	Minimum employee input Management makes decisions ↓
Alienated worker	Empowered worker
Communicates only with supervisor and coworkers	Communicates with employees at all levels and areas

The framework for employee involvement came from the struggle of authentic and inauthentic participation and the degree to which employees have control over their destiny in an organization.

Contemporary Perspective. Current researchers of organizational and human resource development build upon the knowledge of the importance of authentic participation by viewing organizations as systems. These organizations/ systems are then described by systems theorists as dynamic entities that take on a life of their own. According to Katz and Kahn (1966), the theoretical concept of the systems approach begins with input, output, and functioning of the organization as a system rather than with the rational purposes of its leaders. Theorists of this approach believe that the functional whole is more than just a collection of its independent parts and that to understand all aspects of an issue, one must focus on a broad range of factors. For example, to understand the intended and unintended consequences of increased or decreased efficiency, it is necessary to study how pressures to reduce time and eliminate unnecessary activities impact morale, absenteeism, commitment, and employee turnover.

The definition of a system, according to Senge (1990), is a complex set of relationships among interdependent parts or components which illustrate its broad approach in understanding organizational life. At the core of this theory is the notion of systems thinking, which is the conceptual framework for viewing actions in an organization as a whole rather than as isolated events. Systems thinking is a tool for seeing the interrelationships of people and actions rather than linear cause and effect chains. The purpose of this perspective is to enable individuals to shift their minds from seeing parts to seeing wholes, from seeing organizational members as helpless reactors to seeing them as active participants in shaping their reality, and from reacting to the present to creating the future.

Those who interpret organizational life through the systems thinking perspective would view faculty members and all other employees as integral to the institution. Involvement at all levels, staff, faculty, administration, students, is imperative for a highly functioning successful college or university. In this context, involvement is not so much a voluntary "assignment" as a critical aspect of each person's job within the school. The act of decision-making is performed by all and a continuous level of participation and knowledge of the "big picture" is a normal developmental process.

Implicit in this theory is the belief that individuals within an organization are important. Their personal, professional, and team development, coupled with their freedom to interpret and contribute to the greater whole, is the foundation of a successful organization, otherwise termed a learning organization.

Evolution of an Ethical Organization. The ongoing tension that exists between managers and employees serves as a catalyst for continued exploration for the best way to involve employees in the decision-making process. At stake for employees is the intrinsic need to have self-control over their lives, their ability to self-actualize, and acknowledgment for having contributed to the well-being and success of the organization. Fortunately, administrators and leaders of organizations recognize that employee involvement is critical for the success of their product and services in a global economy. Most important, however, is the recognition that employee involvement is not an option; it is the link to an ethical work environment.

Figure 7

Interaction of Worker Alienation and Behavior

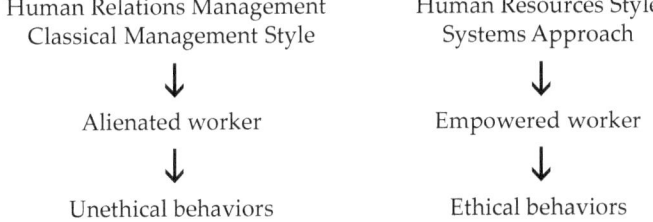

Benefits of Shared Decision Making

When businesses, schools, and other nonprofit organizations function under the assumption that employee participation is an essential ingredient for success, individuals, departments, and organizations on the whole benefit. From the individual to the collected whole, a greater sense of ownership, motivation, and caring emerges as a result of employees contributing their very best to the organization. The following section lists the individual and organizational benefits to shared decision-making. Try to categorize these benefits into structural, leadership, and organizational factors which characterize decision-making processes.

Empowerment: Lack of alienation. Employees are encouraged to do more and do better which involves taking risks and having a greater stake in the success.

Level of Communication: Employees have a clear understanding of how their contribution affects the department and the organization. People are willing to go the extra mile and feel their reputation/name is on the product/service.

Improved Communication: The employee is in the "know" about formal organization information and informal information that is gained through increased opportunities to interact with others. Employees are comfortable communicating horizontally and vertically.

Increased Efficiency: As workers are more cohesive, getting the work done becomes easier and more efficient. Teamwork develops and improves.

Increased Quality: The quality of the product or services improves as personal efficacy increases and employees feel responsible for organizational success.

Higher Work Place Morale: Employees know their input impacts the success of the organization, and this knowledge increases their satisfaction.

Increased Loyalty: With improved morale and quality comes pride and a feeling of ownership.

The Empowerment Issue

When employees have control over their jobs and work environment, it is likely that their overall job satisfaction will increase. Studies have demonstrated that empowered employees miss fewer days of work and make fewer formal complaints than employees who are not empowered. Empowered individuals also chose to remain in their work environment longer than employees who leave due to dissatisfaction and alienation.

The catalyst for improving job satisfaction through empowerment is the practice of open communication. Employees who feel free to express their ideas without fear of retaliation or humiliation tend to be happier than those who are not empowered by open communication.

Empowerment and Risk Taking

Organizations that foster positive change efforts tend to share the same characteristics of organizations that encourage the empowerment of employees. Collegiality, shared goals, and a desire for continuous improvement are common characteristics of organizations that are open to change efforts (Glickman, Gordon, and Ross-Gordon, 1995). A study of empowerment themes (Mallenyzer, 1990) revealed characteristics of empowerment:
- Sharing leadership
- Sharing in decision-making
- Trusting relationships and confidence in self and others
- Extension of recognition and appreciation
- Caring, sharing, and a sense of community
- Honest and open communication
- Collegial and administrative support

When employees are empowered, they are more likely to take risks. They propose new ideas and offer innovative perspectives on issues and problems. These individuals take chances partly because they are in an environment that welcomes opportunities to improve.

Benefits in Academe

Higher education employees and institutions can benefit from shared decision-making practices. This section includes the ways in which faculty life improves when employees are empowered and how that empowerment contributes to the overall well-being of an institution. Try to organize these benefits in terms of group process and communication, group leadership, and organizational criteria.

Institutional affiliation and work motivation
Desire to achieve interaction and subsequent peer affiliation
Increased sense of ownership
Faculty have freedom to develop and manage curriculum, programs, research agendas, etc.
Faculty who view the university/college as a long-term employer
Better attitude toward students and staff
Improved administration of higher education programs: efficiency and quality
Improved communication among key players: faculty and administrators
Ability to attract the best people to the school
Cost savings to the public
Less overlap of programs and policies
Consistency in presentation and implementation
Elevates the reputation of the department within the college
Elevates the reputation of the college within the university which increases resources

The practice of employee involvement and shared decision-making is much more complex than a simple list of do's and don'ts; however, lists do provide a starting point for understanding the relationship among many variables. This section explores the type and origins of barriers that prevent organizations, such as colleges and universities, from offering an authentic context for employee involvement. Again, determine which of these barriers is related to group processes and communication, group leadership, and organizational constraints.

Lack of departmental and organizational mission and goals
Negative culture and climate
Low expectations of individuals
Lack of communication
Lack of trust
Fear of change
There is no perfect model or consensus of the "best" strategy
Preference for the status quo
Time and money
Individual motivation
History of inauthentic participation
High level of willingness but lack of knowhow to mobilize/organize
Unorganized meetings
No faculty rewards (money, recognition, or internal appreciation) for participating in governance activities
No credit for tenure
Faculty often resent the additional work
Faculty often resist the additional work
Some administrators don't think that faculty involvement is totally "good"
The more faculty involved, the slower the decision-making process

Contemporary Research on Faculty Involvement

Although higher education researchers have long investigated issues related to faculty involvement, no particular strategy emerges as the "best" approach for increased decision-making among faculty. This suggests that each institution must develop its unique style, just as groups involved in decision-making processes must examine the best approach for solving each problem.

Current research does lead to three conclusions regarding faculty involvement in higher education. First, the balance of management control and employee participation is as important an issue in higher education as it is in business and profit organizations. Faculty members are highly trained specialists who must be brought into the management of the organization, much the same as frontline employees need to be able to comment and react to assembly line quality. Second, the role and function of faculty and administrators needs to be more clearly defined and communicated. Faculty should be accountable and rewarded for fulfilling their roles and functions. Third, members of the higher education community should prepare for a paradigm shift as some experts foresee the need to radically change the way education is organized.

Empowering Faculty

A recent study (Miller & Seagren, 1993) sought to identify strategies for increasing faculty feelings of empowerment in governance based upon four thematic categories of organizational improvements, administrative changes, culture modifications, and policy amendments. The authors concluded that the organizational structures of higher education institutions often inhibited the quantity and quality of faculty participation. Several strategies to surmount organizational barriers were suggested, including informal social gatherings, participation in state and regional faculty governance organizations, and the opportunity for leadership development. Faculty also reported that traditional management models should be replaced with progressive management models to open channels of communication and collaboration. Within this new model of participation and collegiality, faculty should be rewarded for governance activities through promotion, tenure, and merit decisions.

Recognition and respect proved to be the most important concerns of faculty in the study of empowerment (Miller & Seagren, 1993). Faculty reported that administrators need to acknowledge the importance of their contributions and show respect for their efforts. The results indicate several strategies to benefit faculty and administrators. Administrators' communication and messages should reflect their value of faculty. The role of administrators needs to be clear and should be designed to promote the type of leaders that support joint decision-making. Faculty should be challenged with issues of strategic planning rather than solving short-term, routine problems, and tenure and promotion policies should be amended to accurately reflect the role of faculty.

The Ideal Governance Process

Faculty members identified their perceptions of the "ideal" governance process in a study which examined how faculty from public and private institutions view their participation in governance (Miller, McCormack, & Newman, 1996). Not surprisingly, responses of faculty members from a small private comprehensive university varied significantly from their peers at a large public research-oriented university. On the issue of whether faculty should be rewarded for participation in governance activities, faculty from the private institution were less supportive than faculty members from the larger public university. Perhaps the faculty members at the private school believed that participation is a tradition inherent to their teaching position. Conversely, the public institution faculty members' support of rewards may indicate that the time allocated for tenure-seeking activities such as research is precious, and that in the past their participation has been deemed unimportant or "inauthentic" in nature.

Another area of disagreement among the private and public faculty members in identifying characteristics of the ideal governance process is with the issue of freedom and empowerment to question administrative policy. Faculty at the private institution, which is historically characterized by freedom of expression and participative governance, indicated strong support in the area of questioning the status-quo. However, the faculty members from the public institution were less urgent in their need to question policy. Their responses may be characteristic of those working in a large organization with historically complex and hierarchical decision-making patterns.

Both categories of faculty members were in agreement that in an ideal governance process, the faculty senate is a source for soliciting participation among faculty members, and that involving faculty members early in the decision-making practice is essential. In addition, subjects agreed that faculty have an important role in persuading administrators to value their collective voice.

Improving Organizational Conditions for Faculty Involvement

Many administrators have lamented the fact that it is not possible to mandate a policy that all faculty members will be empowered or that shared decision-making procedures will be in place by next fall. Changing the way decisions are made goes much deeper than policy development or a one-day workshop. For an authentic increase in the level and quality of participation by faculty members to occur, several challenges must be acknowledged and explored by faculty and administrators, beginning with an examination of the existing norms and practices within the organized culture. How do these norms shape faculty attitudes and beliefs? What are the ethical consequences of faculty practices? These questions must be answered prior to determining the extent to which faculty want to increase their role in making decisions. Once participants have shared their beliefs and expectations, then discussions of shared governance goals can lead to actual changes in the way decisions are made and power is shared. This section of the chapter explores staff development topics which facilitate the reform of shared governance.

Change

Those who are involved in, or affected by, a shift in the traditional way of getting things done should be familiar with the predictable reactions and consequences of organizational change efforts. Faculty and administrators should participate in group activities which will allow them to gain knowledge about their own resistance to change and how to cope with new practices and procedures. Informal, facilitator-led sessions could include self-assessment tools to measure personal values and beliefs and to what extent these feelings are flexible. Some people are simply more likely to change their internal makeup than others. In addition, participants should learn about the predictable reactions to change. Specifically, most people move from a self-centered view ("How does this affect me?"), to the actual task ("I'm spending a lot of time in decision-making meetings."), to the impact ("How is this improving instruction and the academic program?").

Both the faculty and the administration may act as change agents in the process of leading the university toward a progressive, participative style of governance. Change agent roles include: catalyst (one who activates change), solution giver (one who has expertise and experience), process helper (one who improves the flow of discussion and debate), and resource linker (one who has financial connections). In addition to taking on the role of change agent, participants should be aware that their capacity for personal vision-building, inquiry, mastery, and collaboration are essential to the success of their change efforts.

Conflict Management

Conflict is an inevitable and consequential component of academic life. Too often, faculty view conflict as something to avoid. Avoiding tough questions and stifling lively debates about controversial issues actually adds to the likelihood that goals will not be achieved. When organizational conflict is managed in a manner that enhances individual, group, and system-wide effectiveness, the likelihood that goals will be achieved is enhanced.

Staff development about conflict management strategies usually center around five styles of handling interpersonal conflict in organizations: integrating, obliging, dominating, avoiding, and compromising. These styles, which were first suggested by Mary P. Follet (Rahim & Blum, 1994), have provided a foundation for measuring and managing conflict. With training, faculty recognize which style they prefer and are able to balance their approach to problems. Additionally, the faculty has a better understanding of how their peers approach conflict.

Communication Skills

Communication researchers have often considered communication style as the organization member's most critical work behavior (Dell, 1992; Weick, 1979). Communication experts such as Weick (1979) and Brandon (1995) report that employee communication must transfer information critical to the organization's success. Further, the style in which critical information is transferred greatly influences the overall success of the interaction. Faculty who are involved in shifting the manner in which important decisions are made must be competent and effective communicators.

Staff development programs present faculty with the opportunity to study their personal communication styles. This is especially critical in developing positive strategies for managing conflict with others. In addition, studying interpersonal communication styles also assists the faculty in becoming sensitive to issues such as gender and race. Being tuned to the behavior of others is an asset when faculty members are negotiating strategies for shared decision-making.

Successful Meeting Skills

How to conduct a successful meeting is a requisite skill for faculty and administrators who chair committees and task forces. The committee leaders should learn about time-saving techniques to implement when planning and conducting meetings. Being prepared and organized sends the message to faculty that their time is valued. Ground rules, such as Seibold's (1992) seven steps for meeting planning, should be established and followed. For example, Seibold suggested:

1. Make sure the meeting is necessary. Often, teleconferencing, electronic mail, and memorandums are sufficient to communicate important information.
2. Identify the specific purpose for the meeting. Determine specific meeting goals. What outcome do you desire?
3. Determine who will attend the meeting. Is this an established committee? Will outside representatives be invited?
4. Finalize the logistics of the meeting. Plan the date and time, location, and refreshments in advance.
5. Establish group roles for those who attend the meeting. Notify faculty in advance if they are expected to take minutes or make a presentation.
6. Always forward an agenda to participants prior to the meeting, this allows for members to prepare for their meeting role.
7. As the chairperson, try to imagine how you want the meeting to proceed. Anticipate potential problems and be prepared to guide the flow and tempo of the meeting.

In addition to learning about how to plan for meetings, faculty should also be exposed to successful meeting formats and procedures. For example, during problem-solving meetings, the chairperson may open the meeting with a brainstorming session or a panel discussion.

Time Management

> This most basic unit and fundamental unit of academic life — the sanctity of the classroom and the authority of the teacher within it— is about to be turned inside out.
>
> William M. Plater

William M. Plater (1995) predicted a new role for faculty in the 21st Century within the context of changing forces in higher education. These major forces, which include technology, accountability, and constituent-based education, are causing change in institutions and highlight an ongoing tension between centralization and decentralization, as well as between standardization and individualization.

Plater forecasted a refocusing of resources which include the recognition that time is the most important resource of faculty. Therefore, the management of time will become a critical issue for managing and excelling in the next decade. Plater offered radical suggestions for the expansion of the variety of faculty roles during the next decade. For example, other employees, such as librarians, technicians, and practitioners, could all compose a 'faculty' team with shared goals related to institutional mission. This type of forecasting, coupled with the organizational change of higher education institutions, dictates that institutions examine and reflect on their current state of decision-making and begin immediate planning on how to become stronger, highly productive organizations.

For Discussion

1. How does having tenure affect and effect a faculty member's willingness to take risks? Can trade-offs for risk taking be negotiated?
2. How would a university benefit, or be hampered, by having a majority of faculty members willing to take greater risks? What if all faculty members increased their risk taking?
3. Describe an organization in which change is viewed as an opportunity rather than as a problem. What are the characteristics of its faculty and administration? Are there external factors which impact this culture?
4. Is your faculty empowered? Are all university employees empowered?

Answer this question using Kanungo's (1992) three-pronged approach:
A. Identify existing organizational norms and conditions that promote or inhibit the work-related behaviors and attitudes of all university employees.
B. Analyze the ethical implications of these organizational norms and the resulting behaviors and attitudes. Do this from the individual's perspective (job satisfaction, productivity) and the organization's perspective (does the university obtain its goals?).
C. Are university practices "good" for the well-being of employees, based on what is considered commonly decent, moral behavior? How can institutional ethics be viewed from both faculty and administrative behaviors?

Section 2

Faculty Co-Governance at Work

Chapter 3
Faculty Involvement in Academic Affairs

by Michael Miller, Richard Newman, and Todd Adams

The management of higher education institutions is based on the concept that effective management strategies enhance or improve the stated mission of the institution, whether that mission be focused on service, research, or instruction. Although the construct may appear simplistic, the range of skills and abilities required for effective academic administration is broad, and at times, nebulous. McCarty and Reyes (1987) in particular noted the complexity and lack of clarity of academic bureaucracy, referring to the lack of a strong foundation in the study of administration and the difficulty in identifying agreed upon outcomes of institutions. Reinforced by Birnbaum (1988), among others, institutions and their leaders consistently encounter difficulty in providing a singular definition of their functions. Despite this, general constituencies in the public see colleges and universities as places where "education takes place."

Regardless of fascination with the Carnegie Classification's ratings, colleges and universities exist to provide opportunities for students to learn. To this end, then, academic quality in its broadest definition is the most important component of the whole. Institutional reputations are vital, and as Bowen (1976) argued two decades ago, all institutions seek prestige and power, and garner all of the resources they can to that end. These reputations have tremendous residual effects, impacting fund raising, relationships with legislators, enrollment, student and faculty retention, and the support necessary to operate in efficient and effective means.

Academic administration's role is concerned with management of the intellectual capital on which reputations are built and maintained. These operations are all encompassing at different times, subsuming faculty efforts in the classroom or laboratory to business operations and facilities which have a relationship to the ecology or inviting nature of the institution. As other sections of this book deal with such areas of effectiveness and athletics, the discussion of academic administration is focused primarily on the role of faculty in working with, and sometimes for, an academic chain of command which places supreme value on reputation.

Academic affairs deals with the offering, structure, rigor, and other issues related to individual and collective academic programs. With many institutions offering over one hundred programs of study, the division typically has a broad span of control which dictates faculty workload, compensation and salary equity, promotion and tenure, and even facility space allocation. Traditionally encompassing strong levels of faculty interest and involvement, these divisions rely heavily on faculty to make decisions regarding admissions, retention, grading, grant writing, and so forth, and must have strong working relationships with faculty groups to ensure academic quality and rigor.

The reliance on faculty by academic administrators raises a vital philosophical question: To what extent are administrative job responsibilities defined to delegate authority to faculty? Most institutions have not clarified this relationship, and consequently, rely on the parameters of the Americans with Disabilities Act, and define the specific relationship between administrators and faculty under the federally mandated concept of "essential functions" (Miles, 1997). Most institutions, however, have not clarified this relationship, and rely on a loose precedent of tradition to defend and explain job responsibilities. Institutions which have implemented bargaining units have a stronger track record of defining expectations of administrators, but even in these settings, the extent to which administrators "grant" faculty the privilege of involvement is suspect. Subsequently, the current chapter was designed to examine the specific actors involved in the academic governance of an institution and explore the current issues which cause concern for involving faculty. Additionally, suggestions are offered to develop a balance between faculty involvement and the current state of academic administration.

Who Is Involved in Academic Governance?

President

The role of the college president is defined by the formal and informal structures of the campus community which respect, or conversely, disrespect, the authority of the position. Although formal job descriptions may define a range of tasks and responsibilities, the ability of the president is reliant on the perceptions of the college's constituents (Fisher, 1984). Birnbaum (1988), Bergquist (1991), and Rosovsky (1990) have defined the effective presidency in terms of an ability to persuade constituents, build coalitions, and provide institutional direction, especially in times of difficulty.

In most institutions the president is in a position to build bridges between those to be involved in the decision-making process. Responsible for the overall working of an institution, the president is reliant on these decision-making parties to collaborate. The president, then, is not only the individual with final authority, but also a team-builder. Difficulties subsequently arise in situations when quick responsiveness is needed and when faculty governance units provide recommendations contrary to presidential vision. An additional major barrier in this situation is that of trust or mistrust between faculty and administrators (Miller & Seagren, 1993).

Frequently, presidential vision is provided initially outside of consultation with faculty. Presidents are hired due to their ability to articulate a vision desired by a selection committee or board of directors, and consensus for this vision is then sifted through various administrative channels to faculty, staff, and students. Such situations compound the difficulties of gaining faculty trust and support, and isolate the president into a relationship of board service.

A further difficulty in presidential leadership related to faculty involvement in governance is the changing nature of hiring and retaining college presidents. At one time the presidential position was the supreme academic leader. As fund raising, board relations, lobbying, and external appearances become increasingly important to colleges, the criteria for selecting a president has changed. Presidents, now more than ever before, are coming from nonacademic positions, such as the corporate setting, business affairs, student affairs, and development, and the result is a changed belief about how faculty are to be involved. Although involvement is generally seen as important, the involvement of faculty and staff is typically considered a procedural issue in decision-making rather than a structural foundation for decision content.

Provost

As the primary academic leader of higher education institutions, vice presidents for academic affairs or provosts are seen as the conduit through which senior administration connects with faculty. Administrative leadership has in fact grown increasingly active, although administrative lines of authority have been seen as muddled and vague. The resultant effect is what Keller referred to as a great leadership crisis (Keller, 1983). The provost position has evolved to take the academic leadership position previously held by college presidents, as virtually all academic matters are channeled through the position. This increase in academic responsibility subsequently requires the direction of and attention to all matters related to academic program planning, development, and evaluation, and in particular, the faculty and various actors who implement these programs.

Faculty Co-Governance at Work 61

What role, then, do those holding the provost position have in governance? In many instances the provost's office serves as the facilitator or clearinghouse for matters related to faculty senates and governance units, often providing agenda items and regular meetings with governance leaders to discuss policy matters and items in need of attention. In a sense, the provost's position creates the climate for respect, trust, and commitment to shared decision-making and the value placed in both the process and the outcome. If a provost refuses faculty input, such an action clearly demonstrates a lack of dedication to shared governance.

Rosovsky (1990) wrote as a rule of governance that not all decisions are enhanced through shared governance and that there are basic differences between the rights of citizenship in a nation and the rights that are attained by joining a voluntary organization. He indicated that the governance process is about power and the disbursement and clarification of who has power. As the primary internal power-broker for the campus, the provost has the ability to define the parameters of internal decision-making and the extent to which decisions are debatable.

Provosts have authority over matters such as faculty workload, compensation, disciplinary excellence, promotion and tenure, and reward structures, and thus maintain control on the matters of most value to faculty. Evaluating programs based on issues such as quality, utility, strengths and weaknesses, and efficiency can also become relevant to the governance process. Should a provost select criteria for assessment, certain disciplines may find difficulty in justifying actions and outcomes. Similarly, program development can be based on internal or external models or designs, and may utilize teams of faculty and agencies such as foundations and trusts which desire to create avenues for problem solving and career development. In either scenario, the academic leader maintains a control to be contested and supported through organized faculty efforts.

Deans

The term "dean" can be traced to the Greek term "seka" and the Latin term "decanus," both of which meant "10," that is, responsibility for ten individuals. In the fourth century, the version of the title, "decania" or "deanery" referred to individuals within the Roman Empire who had responsibility for the burial of the dead. Through evolution, the term came to take on responsibility within religious institutions for the administration of schooling as well as religious activities, commonly claiming a span of control over ten individuals. In German institutions, the position grew to an elected status, as faculty voted for particular leaders, often those with the most seniority, to lead their efforts. Though rarely elected, the term today refers to general academic leaders for specific academic disciplines (Dunn, 1987; Todd, 1965; Ward, 1934).

Similar to other administrative positions, the academic dean has been described sporadically in the literature base, identifying a range of tasks, roles, responsibilities, and challenges. The dean is the singular individual capable of addressing involvement issues from an academic base, serving as a fulcrum of faculty and department chairs to present opportunities and issues for involvement and input. In this capacity, the dean is capable of establishing lines of authority which allow for involvement and policy formation, similar to that of the provost. With responsibility for the academic quality of an individual unit, the dean provides the attention to specific disciplines for enhancement or elimination (Tucker & Bryan, 1988).

Perhaps one of the dean's most difficult tasks is the complexity of providing both internal direction for the unit as well as serving as a strong external liaison with the community, alumni, and potential employers for graduates. Additionally, the dean serves as a faculty member, and thus has responsibility for remaining active in a particular discipline. Combining this state of internal and external responsibility, the dean must be responsive both to the provost on issues of planning and budgeting, but must also serve as a representative of the unit to the senior or central administration.

Deans often make use of a council or committee of department chairs, and at times, also utilize faculty governance units unique to a particular college. Miller (1997B) reported one such instance where a faculty forum served as a type of faculty senate for a college of education. In this situation, all faculty were involved in the creation of college-wide policy and were given an opportunity for direct input into the dean's decision-making. As Miller found, however, this forum rarely drew the majority of faculty to participation, but the assembly did serve as a valuable outlet for faculty to voice concerns and raise issues for discussion.

The dean, as an academic leader, is caught in the middle of channeling faculty desires and visions of program excellence to the mission and picture developed by senior administrators. Through the effective input in decision-making, the dean's position may prove of value to creating an environment of academic integrity within both competing bodies. For self-preservation as well as the welfare of the unit, the dean has a responsibility to involve faculty in creating a vision for the unit, while brokering the attentions and values of senior administration.

Chairs

Of all academic leadership positions, the department or unit chair or head is perhaps in the most precarious position. The chairperson, considered both faculty and administration, has the responsibility of directing college-wide policy to the faculty. Described as "caught in the middle" (Seagren & Miller, 1994) and in the center of a web of responsibilities (Vacik, 1997), the chair acts as a whip to garner faculty involvement, particularly providing attention to the issues and plans developed by deans and senior administrators.

The individual holding the chair position must work to satisfy the needs of deans and senior administrators as those are the people responsible for evaluations and retention in the chair position, but must also work to satisfy the needs of colleagues in the faculty ranks. The chair, an individual who makes approximately 80% of the academic decisions in a college (Creswell, et al, 1990), is influenced by perceptions about career progression and personal life circumstances (Seagren, Wheeler, Creswell, Miller, & Grassmeyer, 1994). Coming from a faculty position, the chair must make the transition from one of autonomy to collective responsibility, and in the process, must consider if the chair position is a way-station to a future in administrative posts, or whether the position serves as a temporary change from faculty duties. Additionally, personal relationships devoted to faculty colleagues may be strained and tested when the chair must take actions which do not support or contradict faculty autonomy.

The analogy of the chair position to the legislative whip has a tremendous impact on how positions and decision-making are implemented. If senior administrators view the chair as one who is responsible for gaining faculty input and developing consensus, then the chair is obligated to serve as consensus and team builder, regardless of particular circumstances. Similarly, faculty may view the chair as their primary advocate, one who will carry their concerns forward in decision-making. In both situations, the chair has a great deal to lose and gain in consensual decision-making.

Program Coordinators

Program coordinators are typically faculty members with partial release time from teaching obligations to conduct the business operations of individual academic programs. Primarily considered faculty, these coordinators have an obligation to participate in governance activities to the extent that they impact their programs, but are also in leadership positions to serve as role models and protectors of academic faculty rights.

Coordinators may view the governance process, in a

broad sense, as a mechanism for manipulating institutional issues to their advantage. In the same vein, these individuals may view governance as an added responsibility without reward or impact on a program, thus rendering involvement as meaningless. Such attitudes have tremendous carry-over impact to program faculty, as the coordinator position typically is representative of the values or mores which guide a programs' growth and development.

At the micro-level, coordinators can see involvement by faculty as a typical matter of doing business; the program can only operate with group input and consensus. At this level, coordinators rely on faculty to be involved in such matters as recruitment, retention, admissions, grade disputes, academic exceptions or bankruptcy, student organization advising, alumni relations, accreditation, and student career placement. At this level, involvement by faculty is a necessity and the program coordinator has ultimate responsibility for input. Failure to gather faculty for such input can be detrimental to a program, resulting in high faculty turnover rates, career burnout, low morale and productivity, decreased student enrollment, and even loss of accreditation.

Issues and Trends

Authority and Accountability

One of the primary issues related to the involvement of faculty in academic matters is that of authority definition. What responsibilities and roles do faculty who are involved have in decision-making? Often, the inability of faculty to directly challenge administrators on issues of defined authority create situations and environments of misunderstanding, neglect, and hostility. If administrative bodies do not view governance units as having a voice in decision-making, policy formation, or policy implementation, then governance units will respond accordingly and behave as organizations without a mission or will spend a great deal of time on procedural issues or matters in which their impact will be minimal.

A corollary to the concept of who has authority is role definition, where "who is held accountable for what?" is the common question. Administrative bodies may view faculty as accountable for instructional quality, while faculty may view developmental efforts which create quality learning environments as the responsibility of faculty development professionals and other administrators. The issue of shared accountability has a more direct relationship to public and funding agency perceptions, as these bodies view from external vantage points the efficiency and ability of an institution to function. The perception of inability to determine internal accountability thus has negative impacts in improving opportunities for increased funding, and subsequently, academic program enhancement opportunities.

Budgeting

Does knowledge of postal or telephone budgets create a more conducive environment for sharing authority? The answer, obviously, is no; however the power gained by knowledge of spending habits and allocations has a great deal to do with the ability of governance units to challenge and respond to administrative bodies. This knowledge can subsequently grow to levels of input and consultation, even control, in creating areas for increased or decreased spending. Budgets serve as a plan for institutional or unit-wide priorities, mapping out where an institution will make a commitment worth the valuable fiscal resource of money.

Faculty involvement in the budgeting process requires attention to broad institutional goals and priorities, as well as discretion, responsiveness, and an ability to see the "big picture" of institutional behavior. One of the primary difficulties in this context is where faculty are, or traditionally have been, in positions of a "watchdog" nature, challenging administrative actions in defense of perceived academic integrity or faculty rights.

Within the realm of budgeting lies an allusion to subsequent issues of trust, mistrust, communication, and authority definition. Who is to have final say in the approved budget? If the faculty role is advisory in nature only, what incentive is there for a) administrators to seek input, and b) for faculty to provide input? The answer to both of these questions is contextual and dependent upon the somehow determined need of the institutional leader to seek input. Depending on the level seeking input, the budgeting process may request direct input through the identification of funding items, priorities, and expected outcomes, or may request indirect input through institutional planning, visioning, creating mission statements and quality criteria, and environmental assessments.

Tenure and Promotion

Perhaps one of the clearest demonstrations of faculty involvement in governance is the right of faculty to decide who is promoted and who earns tenure. This right to select and protect their own is one of the most powerful mechanisms faculty have in dictating the direction, rewards, and workload of faculty. The policy and power has, however, grown increasingly political and at times has been usurped by senior administration. A vision or plan for an institution to become more teaching or research focused, for example, is often proclaimed through administrative channels, yet faculty members are the ones who have the ability to recommend individuals for tenure. Senior administrators, however, have the office-based power to reject or accept these recommendations, thus demonstrating a veto power over faculty. Such power reflects both an ability to support faculty involvement, or conversely, to override and devalue faculty input.

In instances of awarding tenure, faculty involvement typically takes the form of making recommendations. In a sense, then, no real power is demonstrated, although the broad perception of collective faculty voices may pose a threat to administrative bodies. There remains in this process of recommending, accepting, and alluding or threatening to 'veto' a decision, a feeling of cooperation. Rarely on matters of tenure do faculty decisions get overridden, however, on occasion they do. In such instances, the structure as defined in policy manuals and faculty handbooks generally remains one of consultation.

Evaluation

Program evaluation is a fundamental issue in the administrator-faculty relationship and the ability of the two parties to share in decision-making. The sharing of authority in evaluative efforts relies mostly in the identification of criteria for program quality and viability. This criteria can be manipulated to present an academic program as healthy, (for example, high student head count) or used to present low-program quality (for example, an excessively high student-to-faculty ratio).

In voluntary efforts to examine program quality, faculty are typically charged with the majority of the work in collecting and providing the analysis of data relative to program quality, efficiency, and effectiveness. In such environments, faculty have a tremendous opportunity to go beyond traditional recommendations and make statements which demand attention. On the one hand, faculty are placing themselves in a competitive situation with other faculty where the prize may be additional resources. On the other hand, faculty may serve as valuable and creative individuals who can protect their colleagues and programs which may indeed need support and assistance.

Program evaluation is perhaps one of the most important tasks for involving faculty, and the results can be decisive in academic survival. Serving as a tool to build coalitions, this process may either promote campus community or further divide a campus along disciplinary boundaries. Representative bodies, such as a faculty senate, may work to promote collaboration among faculty, yet evaluative efforts have the potential to serve as means for manipulation by administrators of academic programs.

Program Management

Program management is predicated on a set of assumptions relative to how a program is to be implemented. A basic outline for program implementation, then, indicates the identification of a mission or set of goals which frame the objective statements to be created. From these objectives, outcome measures are identified which provide a means for curriculum implementation, the evaluation of actual outcomes, and the systematic evaluation of the program. The process of managing academic programs is reliant on both collective faculty input as well as internal and external community feedback, and perhaps most importantly, a consistency with institutional objectives.

Generally, discussions of academic program management hold central to their discussion the following:

Mission/Goals
    Institutional mission
    College mission
    Department mission
    Department goals

Objective Statements
    College objectives
    Department objectives

Outcomes Measures/Measurement
    Faculty evaluations of students
    Writing and oral communication evaluation
    Student satisfaction surveys
    Student curriculum outcome assessment
    Internship assessment
    Pre-tests
    Post-tests

Exit interview
Alumni surveys
Employee surveys
Professional licensing exam (if applicable)

Curriculum Implementation
Courses
Academic advising
Standing and ad hoc committees
Chairperson's committee
Full-time department meetings
Curriculum committee
Curriculum content areas committee meetings
Internal faculty meeting
Student organizations
Student honor societies

Actual Outcomes Evaluation
Curriculum outcomes

Systematic Department Evaluation
Outcome assessment
Student reports on teaching
Content area review
Annual curriculum and department review
Department advisory committee
Annual faculty evaluation
Annual department report

As a result of the identification of these individual activities, shared governance processes relate most strongly to sharing of work responsibilities and the decision-making at the micro-level which ultimately results in institutional policy and decisions. Another component of program management has to do with the daily responsibilities of brokering work load among a set of faculty while maintaining some degree of leadership responsibility. This delegation of authority is typically not a problem, but can become troublesome when administrators refuse to grant decision-making power to faculty groups, while expecting faculty to work and have input into the implementation of this power.

Student Affairs: An Academic Area?

Purpose of Student Affairs Administration

Student affairs administration, like academic affairs, serves to enhance student learning, albeit in different capacities. Most student affairs practitioners link primary student affairs functions to out-of-classroom activities where they promote co-curricular learning within an institution's educational purpose. Although found in classroom settings (such as student leadership development courses), student affairs administrators are seen most prominently in their involvement beyond classrooms, developing programs and services that bridge curriculum and practical experiences. According to Smith (1982) and Smith and Weith (1985), intellectual achievement is the fundamental mission of colleges and universities. In *A Perspective on Student Affairs*, the National Association of Student Personnel Administrators (NASPA) provided a purpose for student affairs administration and its role in the academic mission:

> Colleges and universities organize their primary activities around the academic experience: curriculum, library, classroom and the laboratories. The work of student affairs cannot substitute for that academic experience. As a partner in the educational enterprise, student affairs enhances and supports the academic mission. (p. 9-10).

Smith (1982) concurred, noting that "student affairs, if it is to be effective and successful, must see itself as part of the institutional mission" (p. 56). To many, the mission of a student affairs division is simple, and as Barr (1997) reported, the goal of student affairs is to create the best possible condition for students to grow and learn.

During an unprecedented era of higher education expansion (1941-1989), student affairs positions were created out of necessity to ease the faculty's increasing responsibilities, in essence, to allow faculty to concentrate on teaching and research (Gardner, 1996). Students have come to demand quality services, inviting campus facilities, health insurance, support for study skills and test taking, financial aid assistance, and among others, an acceptable level of safety on their campuses. With the recession of the early 1990s and the decline in federal and state support for higher education initiatives, institutions are now faced with refocusing on the academic mission while providing the same level of service that students and families have come to expect. Many external to higher education see student affairs as a place ripe for cost savings, and in many instances user-fees have become the coin of the realm, but for the most part, faculty and others on campus are not trained nor willing to accept the functions of the student affairs administrator.

Student Affairs/Academic Affairs Dichotomy

A breakdown between student affairs and academic affairs administrators occurs when the importance of learning outside the classroom and its contribution to the desired institutional goals are not clearly defined or communicated. A common language must be developed between the two divisions that articulates the causes of student learning and further defines what must be accomplished to facilitate this learning (Kuh, 1996A). Collaborative efforts are easier when student affairs divisions are clear with their mission and present a consistent professional orientation (Mitchell & Roof, 1989). The language should not be complicated nor should it be singularly focused on student development theory (Schroeder, Nicholls, & Kuh, 1983). "The goal is to use jargon-free, nontechnical language when explaining to faculty, students, and others the rationale for policies, programs, and practices" (Kuh, 1996a, p. 140). Student affairs functions are often seen as ancillary, and thus faculty view those in student affairs as "activity planners."

Gardner (1996) found several reasons why a chasm exists between student affairs and academic affairs. First, today's academic leaders have not had personal experiences with student affairs administrators, and thus, they do not understand student affairs or perceive it as a serious discipline. Second, on many campuses, students have the lowest status as customers. The highest status seems to be given to those farthest from the students, such as trustees, federal funding agencies, state legislators, media outlets, and administrators with a sense of institutional glory. Student affairs staff are closely tied to the students they serve, and this closeness leads to guilt by association and subsequent neglect until times of crisis. In addition, because student affairs practitioners are often formally trained in education (higher education, counseling), they are seen as less credible because their degree is not in a particular, traditional science or humanities area. Finally, student affairs divisions are seen as competitors for budget dollars to faculty and administrative offices within academic affairs. National publications include reports of cutting student services budgets to protect academic programs and having faculty resume some of the service roles currently provided by student affairs divisions (Cage, 1992; Lazerson & Wagener, 1992).

Like Gardner (1996), Blake (1996) discussed fundamental differences between student affairs and academic affairs after a two-year period involving senior personnel from both divisions. First, personality differences exist between those attracted to student affairs and those interested in faculty positions. Student affairs practitioners take pleasure in collaborating with others, enjoy diversity in people and situations, and celebrate the subjective part of their lives. Faculty, on the other hand, tend to embrace autonomy and the pursuit of knowledge through reflection and ideas, often relying on solitude to accomplish significant findings. Second, the learning that occurs in student affairs differs fundamentally from the learning that occurs in classroom settings. Out-of-class learning is more focused on developing organizational skills and collaborative efforts between groups while classroom learning is highly structured and controlled and primarily focused on individualized learning (Love & Love, 1995). Third, faculty and student affairs practitioners may be seeking contrasting outcomes from their students. Love, Kuh, MacKay, and Hardy (1993) found faculty focused on higher order needs (cognitive development) while student affairs staff focused on both basic (housing, orientation, food service) and higher order (counseling, leadership development, multicultural programming) needs. In fact, student affairs professionals are socialized to de-emphasize cognitive and intellectual development as evidenced in their professional journals (Kuh, et al, 1994). Fourth, and perhaps most significant, each group feels "put down" at times by the other, even during times of cooperation. The battle for turf on the college campus between faculty and student affairs administrators is real, and at times, vicious.

Faculty Involvement in Student Affairs Administration

Informal contact between faculty and students in out-of-class settings has a statistically significant influence on career choice, career interest, and career selection (Astin, 1977; Komarovsky, 1985; Wood & Wilson, 1972). In addition, student contact with faculty beyond normal class interaction is positively correlated with personal growth, leadership, social activism, and intellectual self-esteem (Astin, 1993). Because research suggests positive outcomes with increased student/faculty involvement, student affairs staff continually encourage students to make out-of-class connections with faculty. In addition, activities that involve partnerships or collaboration between student affairs and academic affairs are critical (Brown, 1990). However, how often do student affairs staff foster meaningful relationships with faculty members? The motto, "Do as I say, not as I do," applies here. Student affairs practitioners may also overemphasize the importance of out-of-class activities and communicate to students that classes and lab assignments are somehow less important than organizational leadership roles and campus programs. The danger in overstating the importance of co-curricular involvement by student affairs staff may cause students to "unwittingly diminish" the classroom setting and foster faculty misunderstanding of the role student affairs play (Kuh, 1996b).

Conversely, how many faculty members collaborate with their colleagues in student affairs? Many faculty members believe that classes, laboratories, and other in-class experiences provide the best environment for student learning to occur (Kuh, et al, 1994). Institutional values for faculty include teaching, research, and service (Chait & Ford, 1982). Because these values are normally expressed in tenure and promotion decisions, some faculty find co-curricular activities to be a mild diversion, or even too time-consuming, and thus, the activities serve as a distraction for themselves and their students (Kuh, 1996a).

Ardaiolo (1993) suggested two approaches for involving faculty in student affairs functions, structural and personal. The structural approach has student affairs professionals performing "borderline" duties that could easily be associated with academic affairs, but are located within the student affairs division because of campus history or politics. Admissions, orientation, enrollment management, and retention are examples of areas employing the structural approach to cross-divisional interaction. The personal approach has student affairs staff building relationships with faculty through campus issues, controversies, or crises. Nebraska Wesleyan University employs the personal approach in its weekly forums with scholars lecturing on various topics and current events. Southern Illinois University at Carbondale also utilizes the personal approach by involving faculty in its management team that responds to campus crises.

A seamless learning environment offers a different approach for involving faculty in student affairs functions. A seamless learning environment combines activities assumed to be unrelated (classes and out-of-class experiences) and arranges them to be mutually beneficial and supportive, thereby encouraging student learning (Kuh, 1996b). Although similar to Ardiaolo's (1996) structural approach, a seamless learning environment involves intentionally connecting student affairs and academic affairs through processes (curriculum, experiential learning) that fosters a collaborative effort from both divisions and supports the institutional mission while recognizing students' personal goals. For example, an orientation program that includes academic advising, financial aid counseling, meeting with departmental faculty and staff, campus tours, community service activities, and families create a web of crossing lines between student affairs and academic departments. Inherently, faculty and academic staff are involved (advising, departmental meetings) with student affairs personnel (campus tours, community service activity) to assure a successful transition to college for new students and their families. If a breakdown occurs in planning or implementation between academic and student affairs, overarching institutional goals such as retention and educational success may not be met.

A Balancing Act

The Empowerment Issue

Rosovsky (1990) noted that not all decisions are improved by making them more democratic, and such is particularly the case of instances involving faculty in decision-making. Faculty excel and are noted for their abilities to manage their own professional lives and careers, to motivate those around them through teaching and scholarship distribution, and in the ability to specialize their thinking.

As highly specialized and trained individuals, faculty as a body do not typically tend to agree; they agree to disagree on matters of institutional importance.

Faculty are most likely to display the greatest amount of interest in their power on matters of academic substance. Empowerment related to academic decision-making refers to both the authority and trust demonstrated and given to faculty bodies. In return for this trust, faculty must respond in a timely, responsible, and inclusive manner which illustrates both the desire and nature (seriousness) of academic management. If faculty embrace the opportunity to share authority, then further opportunities are easily opened.

Trust and Mistrust

One of the primary difficulties in effectively sharing authority within the realm of academic affairs is the issue of trust. Senior administrators may have a vision of institutional growth that may not be shared by others, and in the process of developing this vision, the administrators may be seen as forcing their views or ideas on the campus community. This is not uncommon in instances where an external president is hired with promises of creating a research or doctoral granting university atmosphere and standing, regardless of faculty and staff already employed at the institution. Faculty may subsequently view the new administration with mistrust for simple failure to consider the environment and value-structure of the campus prior to making promises about institutional change. Other issues of mistrust by faculty toward administrators may relate to the sharing, or lack thereof, of information and data related to campus issues or concerns.

Administrators may be distrustful of faculty due to such issues as lack of accountability, inability to make decisions quickly, failure to view a senate or representative democracy body as a binding body representative of all faculty, and lack of efficiency. This distrust may permeate all decision-making, and efforts at shared authority become forums for placation, allowing faculty to merely voice their concerns with no real possibility of impacting policy formation.

Communication and Propaganda

The ability to involve faculty is dependent on the processes and content of communication which is jointly shared. If budgetary information is only partially released, for example, faculty may be less responsive when called upon to make recommendations for program restructuring. Virtually all institutions make use of some form of faculty and staff newsletter, magazine, or newspaper to communicate a weekly or monthly "state of the campus," position openings, and notes about faculty and staff. However, this mechanism often fails to provide the information needed for effective involvement. If administrators can rely on data provided by institutional research, then so should faculty.

Information presented through public forums takes two roles: opinion manipulation and information. The difficulty in regard to faculty governance is to identify what information conveyed from senior administration is informational. Then, what information from senior administration is provided in hopes of bringing the campus community in-line with the thoughts and desires must be determined. Since administrators have control of university relations, development, and alumni relations offices, they naturally have an infrastructure which can comply or be manipulated at their behest. Administrators can often establish formative channels to "tell the story" of the institution, programs, and so on. Although this is a tremendous institutional strength, it does present difficulties for faculty bodies which do not have similar capabilities for either generating or disseminating views which may contrast those of campus officials.

Seeking Success

Florida International University (FIU) (1997) provided a key to creating an environment of effective, quality shared governance. The FIU criteria consisted of three simple, yet important, considerations for building the involvement of faculty:

> Identify Key Faculty
> Recruit Quality Faculty
> Win Over Faculty

The criteria encouraged the selection of faculty leaders from the campus community, including well-respected scholars, leaders in involvement, campus-wide committee chairs, those willing to question administrators in public forums, and so on. This criteria encouraged the involvement of faculty who are already seen as holding leadership positions.

Another popular method for working to achieve better results has to do with clarifying role expectations and lines of authority. This technique, often expressed through the use of flowcharts, allows for the specific identification of who is responsible for specific tasks and duties. Flowcharts are often utilized as illustrations for work responsibility rather than tools for defining responsibility. If flowcharts are applied in a realistic fashion, there is greater clarity established about who does what, and what the boundaries are for making decisions and taking responsibility for individual actions.

A host of business practices can be alluded to in referencing effective academic administration. Blanchard (1997) argued for a process of effective management which focused on having a product that works, quality people, a passion for what you do, a sense of urgency in everything you do, providing outstanding customer (student) service, having faith in yourself, and relying on money as a product of some other success. According to this set of criteria, administration finds success not in working to define or restrict faculty, but rather, in focusing on serving the various constituencies of the institution.

One of the more daring and visible means for faculty to keep administrators in check is the University of Colorado at Boulder's administrator rating. On an annual basis, administrators are rated based on their performance by those who work for them and by the faculty, in situations where administrators, in a sense, report to the faculty. A sample of this type of rating is provided for discussion in Appendix 3.

The intent of this chapter was not to strengthen the argument of the faculty versus administration, but rather, to highlight areas of potential conflict and disagreement. The power of faculty to be involved in meaningful academic and institutional change is very real, and has been demonstrated on occasion throughout history. For example, faculty involvement in the academic freedom movement of the 1960s made fundamental changes to higher education in the early 1970s.

For Discussion
1. To what extent is academic leadership responsible for soliciting and rewarding faculty involvement? If involvement is to be valued, what can those in leadership positions do to recognize this commitment?
2. As efforts are directed at reforming tenure privileges through post-tenure evaluations and continuing contracts, what role do faculty have in deciding criteria for evaluation?
3. What meaningful, substantive changes have faculty governance units made during the past decade? Are these adequate to continue justifying faculty participation? If not, what kinds of specific outcomes from involvement are necessary?
4. How are those involved in faculty governance units capable of gaining access to information utilized to make academic program decisions? Does this access differ from administrators' channels, and if so, should the channels differ?
5. Should faculty involvement in academic affairs differ from the format or process used to involve faculty in nonacademic matters? What advantages and disadvantages can be identified in relation to faculty having ownership of academic programs?

Chapter 4
Faculty Involvement in Athletic Administration

by Richard E. Newman and Jane G. Bartee

The emphasis placed on college athletics has grown to unprecedented levels due largely to the ability of "college sports" to generate revenue, especially among the NCAA's Division I elite football and basketball powers. With this increase in attention, serious questions have arisen concerning the most effective way to internally regulate college athletic programs.

Most major college sports programs employ an athletic director, as well as several assistant or associate directors, to oversee specific activities or functions such as sports and media information, fund raising, compliance, academic support/counseling, and contest management. In spite of this regulatory system, incidences of abuses, irregularities, student payments, and academic misconduct have frequently been reported by the media. Perhaps the traditional regulatory paradigm of college athletics is insufficient to properly control current athletic programs. It may be that other check and balance measures are necessary to guide or channel athletic programs in an ethical, positive, and meaningful direction.

The work of any faculty is carried on in large part by the action of various committees. As such, committees are constituted to provide a forum through which in-depth attention can be devoted to tasks and matters that affect an institution's program offerings as well as its students, faculty, and staff. Consequently, most faculty committees are empowered to conduct investigations, make recommendations, and formulate policy and legislation on matters under the umbrella of their jurisdiction.

A college or university's faculty athletic committee offers no exceptions to the committee scope and purpose functions in general. The composition of a faculty athletic committee varies, but normally it is comprised of an athletic director, a conference and national affiliation representative (faculty athletic representative or FAR), a select number of faculty members, and an assortment of students.

In terms of functions, most faculty athletic committees are charged with the following duties: (1) displaying accountability for the adherence and enforcement of all conference and national organization rules and regulations; (2) reviewing, evaluating, and providing guidance to the institution and administration on the overall athletic program; (3) providing input regarding the addition or replacement of coaching personnel; (4) policy formulation; and (5) maintaining a framework of academic integrity within the athletic program.

Academic integrity has been cited as one of the benchmark elements underlying current reform efforts in intercollegiate athletics (Knight Foundation Commission on Intercollegiate Athletics, 1991; 1992; 1993). Academic integrity is a complex issue which implies that student-athletes are students as well as athletes from the time of their matriculation to the point of their departure from campus. Inherent in academic integrity is the belief that it must apply to admission policies, to satisfactory academic progress, and to graduation rates.

The importance of academic integrity was aptly depicted by the level of emphasis it received in the Knight Foundation's Commission on Intercollegiate Athletics model of reform, "One-Plus-Three" (Knight Foundation Commission on Intercollegiate Athletics, 1991). Academic integrity was recognized as an integral part of the model because "intercollegiate athletics must reflect the values of the university" (p. 11). Athletic participants must be students, first and foremost, and the entire issue of the athletic reform movement is the "fundamental issue of grounding the regulatory process in the primacy of academic values" (p. 11).

Controlling College Sports

Historical Control Measures

A struggle over the appropriate control of intercollegiate athletics existed from 1874 to 1898. Faculty control of athletics and the concept of faculty athletic committees emerged during this era because of "the inability or unwillingness of students to control their own athletic programs" (Smith, 1983, p. 372). These early internal regulatory efforts were not consistently effective because of the philosophical differences between students and faculty regarding various program elements. However, the efforts did establish a trend toward institutional control of athletic programs.

Academic leaders in the late 1800s also produced the first attempts at interinstitutional regulation of athletic programs. Efforts were hampered by philosophical differences between leaders at various institutions, but the attempts did produce some guidelines that had significant implications for the future. Eligibility standards, academic integrity, amateurism, and role and mission charges affixed to faculty athletic committees can all be traced to this era, and specifically to the Brown Conference Report of 1898 (Smith, 1983).

A wake of reform in intercollegiate athletics in the United States surfaced with what has been referred to as the 1905 football controversy. Two opposing factions, the Intercollegiate Athletic Association of the United States and the Intercollegiate Football Rules Committee, met with controversy over restrictions to place football in its "proper perspective," the spirit of rules, and the explicit authority to establish and regulate rules (Lewis, 1975). The controversy, cited as "the single most important event in the history of intercollegiate sport" (p. 202), required mediation efforts by President Theodore Roosevelt and eventually led to the establishment of the National Collegiate Athletic Association in 1910.

Roosevelt's role in this reform effort has never been

completely clarified. According to Lewis (1975), the President was neither reformer nor abolitionist. He "used his position in government and his personal power of persuasion" (p. 203) to force the Intercollegiate Football Rules Committee to recognize the Intercollegiate Athletic Association of the United States. Subsequently, in 1906 the members of the Association adopted a constitution and bylaws. Armed with neither legislative nor executive powers, the Association advocated faculty control of athletic programs within its member institutions and exhorted the educational value inherent in athletics. "Four years later the name of the Association was changed to the National Collegiate Athletic Association. Thus, President Roosevelt should properly be viewed as one of the founding fathers of the National Collegiate Athletic Association" (p. 202-203).

A second perceived need for change in America's intercollegiate athletic programs prompted a Carnegie Corporation study, conducted under the direction of Howard J. Savage in the mid 1920's (Hanford, 1979). The three-year investigation produced a document that "traced the development of college sports and described the unhealthy state of intercollegiate athletics" (p. 353) in higher education institutions.

Within the context of the Savage report was a key theme which suggested that "defense of the intellectual integrity of the colleges and universities lies with the president and faculty" (Thelin & Wiseman, 1989, p. 64). Savage's recommendations for change were largely ignored, as they ultimately "had little effect on the direction in which men and events were moving intercollegiate athletics" (Hanford, 1979, p. 353).

Intercollegiate athletics reform remained in relative obscurity until the early 1950's. Concerned about a possible overemphasis on major college sports and the maladies caused by the point-shaving scandals in men's basketball programs, an American Council on Education (ACE) committee conducted an inquiry into the nature of college sports

(Hanford, 1979). The ACE Committee, comprised of college chief executive officers, ultimately decided that "presidential action was needed" (p. 354) to combat a general, but valid concern relative to an overemphasis on sports in higher education. The committee concluded its mission with a set of recommendations aimed at resolving some of the perceived problems in "big-time," revenue-generating college sports. These recommendations, however, were ignored by the people or forces directing the fate of college athletics.

Following a second examination of intercollegiate athletics, the Commission of Collegiate Athletics of ACE developed three policy statements pertaining to the role and responsibilities of athletic directors, presidents, and trustees for the conduct of collegiate athletic programs. Funded by the Ford Foundation, the commission was mandated to examine the state of American collegiate athletics and "prepare conclusions and recommendations that would aid in their management" (American Council on Education, 1979, p. 345). The commission's position advocated the need for athletic programs that enhanced the primary educational mission of the institution and that were directed by clearly defined, well-formulated institutional policies. The elements of integrity and ethics were repeatedly emphasized in all three of the commission's policy statements.

The National Collegiate Athletic Association (NCAA), according to Toner (1984), "was formed in answer to public criticism and national concern about a lack of control at institutions of higher education" (p. 13). Since 1906, the Association has advocated the principle that "athletics must be conducted as an integral part of the dignity and high purpose of higher education" (p. 13).

Proposition 48, a by-product of the ACE's Commission on Collegiate Athletics (Zingg, 1983), was initially introduced as a "reasonable minimal level of academic qualifications for freshman eligibility" (Toner, p. 14). The measure was designed to address the issue of academic integrity and "was created, in part, as an effort to quell the mounting controversies surrounding the academic deficiencies of scholarship athletes and questionable academic practices of big-time college athletic powers" (Ervin, Sounders, & Gillis, 1984, p. 15). The standard represented an isolated legislative effort supporting the cornerstone principles of the NCAA.

Proposition 48 was preceded by two other NCAA standards aimed at academic integrity. In 1965, the NCAA adopted the "1.600 Rule" which required college bound high school athletes to achieve a predicted first-year college grade point average of at least 1.600 (C-minus) before they could receive athletic scholarship assistance (Dealy, 1990). During its six-year life, "the measure noticeably improved the academic caliber of the NCAA athletes" (Dealy, p. 112).

A "2.00 Rule" was enacted by the NCAA in 1971 and was theoretically intended to be more stringent than the "1.600 Rule," but proved to be more permissive. The 2.00 Rule required an athlete to have graduated from high school with a C+ or 2.0 grade point average in any combination of courses, rather than a specific core group of courses. Consequently, "the NCAA weakened rather than strengthened the academic standards of its athletes" (Dealy, p. 112) because the admission of marginally prepared student-athletes was virtually unregulated. Phelps (1982) concurred, noting "the graduation rate for the student-athlete has been decreasing consistently since the removal of the 1.600 rule" (p. 14). Proposition 48, in essence, was a "reaction to the fact that colleges had stepped out of bounds on the admissions of unqualified student-athletes" (Cramer, 1986, p. K1).

The NCAA legislatively permitted a form of "open enrollment" for student-athletes from 1971 until the implementation of Proposition 48 in 1986. Academic standards had eroded to the point where an increasing number of underprepared student-athletes were gaining admission to colleges; many of these scholarship athletes were "unqualified young men who had no chance, not in the classroom and not for a degree" (Underwood, 1980, p. 41).

Current Control Measures

Research led Sperber (1990) to conclude that the hypocrisy and fiscal irresponsibility associated with 'big-time' college sports represented a "situation that is untenable for American higher education, and a basic redefinition of the role of intercollegiate athletics within the university is absolutely necessary" (p. K2).

The task of reforming intercollegiate athletics is complex, and the processes necessary to enact change are multiple. Certain recurring themes, however, permeated the literature and indicated measures to strengthen institutional control of athletic programs.

Grant (1979) contended that there has been an erosion of institutional control of intercollegiate athletic programs and that institutional authority must be reestablished. Atwell (1991) voiced similar feelings in his regulatory approach to reform versus deregulation. His approach entailed more institutional control by campus chief executive officers as well as the cooperative support and active involvement of a concerned faculty. He claimed that "faculties have forfeited their role as guardians of academic values" (p. 10), and there is a legitimate need to "regain faculty interest in the oversight of intercollegiate athletics" (p. 11). The primary role of the faculty was viewed as being a defender of "the centrality of the academic enterprise" (p. 11), and as such, they should be involved in delineating "what role organized sports do or should play in a holistic academic enterprise subsuming both curricular and co-curricular activities" (p. 11).

Weistart (1987) mentioned some alternative intervention agencies that might play a part in the current reform efforts targeted at major college athletics. Aside from increased academic standards and closer institutional oversight or supervision, the NCAA, Congressional involvement, and accrediting organizations were mentioned as possible agents needed to enact major reform efforts in intercollegiate athletic programs. He claimed accrediting organizations held particular promise for change because they were in a position to establish academic standards, to require meaningful reporting of academic statistics, or to threaten suspension from accreditation should institutions or institutional programs neglect to satisfy their accreditation standards.

The Knight Foundation's Commission on Intercollegiate Athletics (1991) echoed many of the sentiments on sports reform expressed by Weistart (1987) when it adopted its new model for intercollegiate athletics. Entitled "One-Plus-Three," the model's principle component of "one" centered around the establishment of presidential control of athletic programs. Presidential control, in turn, would be directed toward "three" critical issues surrounding the current sports reform movement: academic integrity, financial integrity, and independent certification.

Implementation of the Knight Commission recommendations need the support and approval of a body possessing the legislative power or authority to enact change. Impetus for change was provided by the Presidents Commission of the NCAA, college and university presidents, and governing boards (Knight Foundation Commission on Intercollegiate Athletics, 1992). The academic integrity reform measures and proposals incorporated into the Commission's study were formally enacted by NCAA protocol during its 1992 convention. The NCAA's member institutions approved measures and proposals aimed at higher academic standards by a 3-1 margin. In essence, this event signified that presidential control of college sports programs was beginning to emerge. The primary focus of CEO control was immediately directed by legislative controls designed to promote the concept of academic integrity in intercollegiate athletic programs.

Dickason (1979) presented a projected view of collegiate athletics for the year 2000. His predictions were based on the opinions, views, and forecasts of the American Council on Education's seven-member Commission on Collegiate Athletics and eleven of its liaison representatives.

The regulation of athletics rendered some futuristic projections that were clearly aligned with some of the current reform discussions. For example, regarding college athletic programs and possible governmental intervention, Dickason wrote:

> Unless the voluntary associations (NCAA, NAIA, and NJCAA) are more successful than in the past, federal government regulations will affect, and possibly interfere with the administration of collegiate sports activities. Government cannot do it better, but government will do it more unless extraordinary efforts by the associations are made to resolve differences and proceed with a rational resolution of these concerns (p. 506-507).

Sharing Authority Effectively

On the part of athletic administration in concert with institutional administration, athletic program effectiveness must be addressed. Specifically, athletic administrators need to understand the impact of involving or not involving their faculty colleagues in athletic decision-making and policy formation. Athletic program offerings, in a general sense, serve as an auxiliary function of the institution and were originally conceptualized to provide for student growth, development, and socialization. The current emphasis, however, has been to utilize athletic programs as both symbols of institutional quality and pride, and as mechanisms for generating revenue. As of the mid 1990's, however, only a handful of athletic programs had proven to be financially solvent on a consistent basis. In order for athletic programs to be effective and successful, specific attention must be directed at the avenues of enhancing and enriching both institutional image and institutional quality.

Positive Impacts of Faculty Involvement

Faculty, as a collective body of professionals and individually, expressed negative attitudes and perceptions in regard to collegiate student-athletes (Engstrom, Sedlacek, &

McEwen, 1995). Faculty have expressed significantly different views toward student-athletes as compared to traditional undergraduates, often believing that student-athletes receive special recognition and attention. Faculty members have also regarded student-athletes earning strong grades with suspicion, and have often felt "angered and embarrassed" (p. 222) by giving such a grade to a student-athlete. Such resentment on the part of faculty is not necessarily their own fault, but rather, may be a symptom of the institutional culture where athletics and success in competition are valued equally, if not more, than the academic achievements of traditional students.

Increasing the involvement of faculty members in the decision-making process of athletic department policy may, in part, reduce the negative attitudes of faculty toward student-athletes. This effect could result in a more favorable educational climate for student-athletes and afford the potential for a quality education. Increasing the sense of empowerment of faculty in the policy making process of athletics may also be beneficial in reducing, or perhaps even eliminating some of the negative attitudes faculty members harbor toward student-athletes. The reduction of negative faculty attitudes could result in a more positive educational experience for the typically sports-minded student-athlete. If student-athletes sense their instructors hold positive attitudes toward them, the result may be better grades, more and better classroom and campus participation, and an increase in student learning. All of these results may subsequently have residual effects on other constituents in the learning environment.

Student-athletes are both loved and hated by their fellow students (Zingg, 1982), and stereotyping of the "dumb jock" may possibly be reduced by increasing faculty involvement. When there are fewer negative attitudes focused on the student-athlete, other students are less likely to focus on their own negative perceptions of the student-athletes. Thus, faculty involvement may abet an improvement of the

general attitude toward the student-athlete.
 In such a scenario, the athletic program certainly benefits, but what about the impact on faculty? Faculty members choose their institutions based on academic discipline, reputation, geographic location, and a host of other real and perceived benefits from institutional affiliation. By enriching these variables, the potential for faculty longevity and morale are poised to improve.

Non-Involvement Impacts
 Negative ramifications could occur if faculty are continuously omitted in the formulation of regulations and policies by the athletic department which pertain to student-athletes. Some faculty members already house more negative attitudes toward student-athletes than they do toward students in general (Engstrom, Sedlacek, & McEwen, 1995). If these negative attitudes from faculty are not rectified and improved, the educational experience of the student-athlete will be less enjoyable and meaningful. The classroom will become a place of stress, detracting from both the physical and mental performance of the student-athlete. In addition, stereotyping of student-athletes by other students will be reinforced by faculty as they portray their negative attitudes toward the student-athletes in the classroom, thus alienating the student-athlete more from the general population.
 Continued noninvolvement of faculty may also further isolate the athletic department in the higher education enterprise, segmenting the emphasis on what athletic practices are effective and noneffective, and placing more value on what successes the athletic teams have. The isolation of athletic programs has the potential to greatly divide a campus into factions of support and nonsupport, particularly if the institution participates in high-profile and revenue-producing athletics. The NCAA, in Article 4, (Organization) of their 1996-1997 Manual of the National Collegiate Athletic Association (1996), specifies a Faculty Athletic Representative. This representative, however, is not defined as a full-

time faculty member, but rather, is identified as a faculty member or administrator who is not an employee of the athletic program. Such a failure to specify an instructional staff member creates a means for senior- and upper-level administrators to continue an overemphasis on winning teams and revenue production. In many cases, college deans and directors are appointed to serve as the "faculty" athletic representative, thus furthering the division between instructional practices, the classroom, and the playing field.

Involving Faculty: Methods for Collaboration

Accepting the premise that faculty should be involved in athletic administration, a serious dialogue is needed between the faculty and athletic leadership personnel concerning expectations, methods, rewards, and functions. As is the case at many institutions, and as argued by Birnbaum (1988), faculty committees are often formed when objectives and outcomes have previously been determined. As literature and professional experience indicates, there is some natural distrust between the athletic and academic camps on college campuses, and perhaps building trust between these groups is the most important initial building block to sharing authority. In addition to building trust, five methods for building collaboration between faculty and athletics are suggested for discussion.

1. At the University of Nebraska-Lincoln, the Athletic Department sponsors an end of the year academic banquet for academically successful student-athletes (GPA over 3.0), where student-athletes can invite one of their teachers from the current semester. Often inviting a favorite teacher, the relationship between the athlete and faculty member becomes strengthened, and subsequent feelings of animosity are diminished. At no expense to the faculty member, athletes and faculty members are provided with an insight into the workings of an athletic program, and a potential exists

for stronger ties by faculty to the athletic program and even ownership into the intricate functioning of the athletic program.

2. Shared authority must be based on improved inter-campus communication, both flowing to and from faculty constituencies to athletic administrators. Many institutions utilize a Task Force for Athletic Integrity, a committee comprised of volunteer, full-time faculty who meet monthly to discuss both current issues and athletic department policy. Although the task force concept works only to the extent allowed by athletic forces, the involvement of faculty allows athletic administrators an opportunity and venue for developing collaborative relationships and enhancing program quality. Other similar concepts include the creation and distribution of a newsletter published by the athletic department which shares information about athletics, student-athletes, and focuses on the academic achievement and processes/environment of student-athlete learning. A semiannual town hall meeting among interested faculty and athletic department personnel also allows faculty and students an opportunity to discuss important issues and feelings. Functioning as an open-house event, faculty (specifically NOT administration, staff, alumni, and boosters) are provided with an opportunity to meet informally with coaches and athletic-administrators concerning academic matters or other topics of concern.

3. The development of an institutional policy which protects faculty from being pressured or coerced into providing specific, inflated grades to student-athletes. Pressure for grades often comes from individuals affiliated with revenue producing sports, and normally results from a desire to keep "key" student-athletes eligible. This policy, however, can not be mandated by senior level administrators, but should be developed naturally through a forum or senate, where diverse academic disciplines have the opportunity to interact with athletic personnel in crafting a protective policy of academic freedom in reference to athletics. In

such an instance, the process of drafting and adopting a formal policy does as much to protect and inform faculty and athletic administrators as it does once it is adopted (e.g., the process of sharing authority is as important as what authority is shared).

4. Athletic departments should become more open to involving larger numbers of faculty, along with valuing this involvement. Similarly, faculty governance groups should make objective, meaningful efforts to participate with athletic-related issues. In developing a more constructive, meaningful dialogue between the two groups, a "valued-added" partnership can produce a host of policies, practices, and perceptions which benefit the institution, the institutional climate or environment, and the athletes. Growing beyond the NCAA mandate of one Faculty Athletic Representative, athletic partnerships on campus can lay the ground work for a long-term overhaul of the role of sports in higher education.

5. Athletic programs should make every effort to identify and recruit key faculty members to participate in their governance. By looking for leaders in faculty senates or academic departments, identifying those who serve on key institutional committees, and by finding those who are esteemed by their students and colleagues, athletic programs can be more efficient and effective in developing a platform of mutual trust with the academic affairs of the institution.

A number of potential, positive benefits can be derived from greater faculty involvement in athletic administration. Tensions and negative attitudes toward athletics, administrators, and student-athletes will be reduced with a greater understanding of each other. Faculty involvement can be of crucial importance to athletic administrators as well as faculty, as issues such as student recruitment, advising, and satisfactory academic progress can all be aided with the input and assistance of faculty. The stereotyping by faculty members and the general undergraduate student body toward student-athletes can be curtailed through the increased interaction by both faculty and administrators, making the undergraduate experience more meaningful for all. Current trends toward the production of revenue through athletics will continue until athletic programs voluntarily take steps to involve other campus constituents in the policy and decision-making process. These steps can represent long-term initiatives which potentially can heal the separatist attitudes which exist on so many of today's college and university campuses.

For Discussion

1. What institutional impact can faculty have on athletic program development? Does this impact alter or change the policy formation structure of an athletic program? Should it?
2. How does an institution appoint members to athletic program advisory or oversight boards? To what extent should a Faculty Senate or Forum be involved in filling this appointment?
3. What is or should be the mission of a faculty member appointed as the NCAA Faculty Athletic Representative? How should this individual represent and inform the faculty body?
4. Do revenue producing sports dramatically alter the perceptions of student-athletes and athletic departments? Would institutions be better off if sports were divided into revenue producing and nonrevenue producing sports? Can revenue producing sports be separated from the institution, while still remaining administratively (or traditionally) linked? Can private college and university foundations take control of revenue producing sports?
5. How does an institution effectively manage a revenue producing sports program? What role should faculty play in this management?

Chapter 5
Faculty Involvement in Institutional Fund-Raising

by Thomas A. Bila

During the past two decades, colleges and universities have come to rely greatly on fund-raising efforts to replace or augment existing sources of revenue. In many instances, state appropriations have been reduced or have been static in growth, while in private institutions dramatic tuition increases have not been able to adequately combat rising operational costs. In both instances, reliance on fund-raising activities and endowment income has been transformed from providing a "margin of excellence" (Hoeflich, 1987), to providing a means of survival. The result has been increased amounts of money raised by higher education institutions as well as a greater institutional attention to the mechanisms for raising this money (Smith, 1996).

Market research for higher education fund raising has been inclusive in relating giving to undergraduate experiences, demographic trends, personality characteristics, giving ability, and frequently, the process of soliciting contributions (Bila, 1992; Connoly & Blanchette, 1986). Research into effective fund raising has even centered on faculty as donors, revealing that faculty provide financial contributions based on their positive feelings toward their employing institution (Holland, 1997).

The process of raising money, as alluded to by the growing body of literature, is a complex process based jointly on donor motivation, communication, belief in the cause or case, and the process in which these are combined to form a solicitation (Rowland, 1986). This process of solicitation typically takes the form of a professional fund-raising executive, such as a "development officer," but has more typically employed entire divisions for fund raising, ranging from professionals dedicated to donor research, annual gifts, major gifts, deferred gifts, capital campaigns, stewardship, alumni and cultivation activities, and record keeping.

To guide how faculty become involved in this process of raising institutional money, several fundamental terms related to fund-raising activities must be defined:

Annual Giving: an amount of money or service given annually; a fund-raising program that generates gift support on an annual basis. Typically, these are a multitude of $25 and $50 gifts which are spent on immediate institutional needs.

Capital Campaigns: an intensive fund-raising effort to meet a specific goal within a specified period of time for one or more major projects that are out of the ordinary, purchase of equipment, or the acquisition of endowment funds. Although increasingly common, these campaigns are usually conducted every seven or ten years, and require a substantial institutional commitment.

Major Gifts: a significant contribution, dependent upon the size, scope, and expectations for an institution. Many institutions will consider a gift in the $25,000 range "major;" however, many large and prestigious private institutions will consider "major" gifts only those in the million dollar range.

Planned Giving: a systematic effort to identify and cultivate a person for the purpose of generating a major gift that is structured and that integrates sound personal, financial, and estate-planning concepts with the prospect's plans for lifetime or testamentary giving. A planned gift has tax implications and is often transmitted through a legal instrument, such as a will or a trust (Levy & Cherry, 1996).

These gift types have traditionally be conceptualized in a pyramid structure which defines a base of support as annual gifts (see Appendix 4). The pyramid concept holds that annual gifts and activities, such as volunteering for homecoming events or hosting athletic receptions, are the entry point for future major donors. The role of the development officer, then, is to utilize a combination of marketing, research, communication, and personal investment strategies to move the entry-level donor to more substantial (higher gift) levels.

Although some may argue that involvement of faculty in fund raising should be treated as an issue separate from governance, there must be consideration given to the concept that fund raising is broadly revenue generation. The generation of this income often allows institutions to pursue agendas of promise or interest, and in this pursuit, institutions create a niche or unique market and notoriety for themselves. In a sense, the obtaining or financial resources has everything to do with institutional governance.

Who Raises Money?

Work in alumni and development relations necessitates a significant commitment of time in building relationships and trust between the institution and the alumni and friends of the institution. Unless the development and alumni officers have been part of the institution for some time (either as employees or as students and now alumni), they need the support and assistance of a strong board of trustees, a strong president, and a loyal faculty and staff. Although this seems expected, some institutions do not actively seek to involve the faculty, staff, administration, and board of trustees in all development and alumni activities, and consider the process an informal, family-type activity rather than a multi-billion dollar industry.

Nearly two generations ago, the increase in fund-raising campaigns as well as the increase in the number of development officers at colleges and universities was noted in the *Greenbrier Report:*

> In the years since the Second World War, a new ad-

ministrative area in higher education has emerged. It is an area which does not even have a commonly understood name, as yet; it is sometimes called university (or college) relations, and sometimes a man rather than a job is given a title and simply called assistant to the president...The precise dimensions of this area also lack definition. Some of its components are clear at first glance, however; it obviously includes public relations, alumni relations, and fund raising. (1965, p. 31)

Research has indicated that to be successful and to assist in the long-term advancement of the institution, an alumni relations or development officer must remain at the institution for a minimum of three years (Bailey, 1988); however, development officers frequently leave before this three-year stay is completed (Bila, 1992). Bailey indicated that it takes this long to adequately determine institutional needs, to analyze the mission, to state the institutional case, and to win friends and contributions for the institution. Research continues to demonstrate (Panas, 1988) that the average development director remains at an institution for eighteen months and then moves to another location, either by choice or by the request of senior-level administrators.

Literature and professional programs have suggested that many alumni and development officers remain at an institution for a short period of time due to employer or institutional expectations which are unrealistic. Heuerman and Spitaels-Ginser (1985) suggested that professional organizations such as the NSFRE and the Association for Healthcare Philanthropy (AHP) must stress to employers that

> 1) Development and alumni relations are long-range projects and it's in the best interest of the institution to have a stable lengthy relations with the development/alumni officers;
>
> 2) Fund-raising goals must be set based on the needs and setting of each institution — one institution's miracles may be another's bane; and

3) Development and alumni officers each have different areas of expertise and different sources of funding, so it is important to choose the one who can best address the sources in the community. (1985, p. 10)

A common concern among higher education development officers is how to involve faculty in the identification, cultivation and eventual solicitation of alumni and friends of the institution, and how to use their expertise in building relationships between their former students and the institution. In addition to successfully collaborating with faculty to raise institutional support, development administrators can play a key role in helping faculty renew acquaintances with previous favorite students and can assist in institutional growth through the utilization of faculty to "paint pictures" of academic quality and the future in specific disciplines. The involved faculty member provides the stamp of authenticity which often makes a major difference in giving.

Of all individuals on campus, in dealing with donors as well as alumni, faculty members can be the most influential. From their classes and frequent interactions with students, long-term relationships can be constructed or destroyed. From the faculty member's teaching abilities and skills, students are inspired, and these points of interaction provide the rich fabric necessary for development officers to weave together a story of institutional need and promise. This is typically referred to as the statement of need or case for support.

A Basic Fund-Raising Philosophy

To better frame how faculty can be and are effectively involved, several principles for fund raising must be addressed. These principles are based generally on the growing research into fund-raising effectiveness, and specifically on the professional dialogue which has created a tightly-focused body of professional associations. They may vary based on institution, but generally can be accepted as guiding principles to raising money.

Guiding Fund-Raising Principles
1. People give to people;
2. People want the "happy experiences" or good feelings that giving to others provides;
3. People want to help the institution meet its needs and strengthen its mission;
4. Partnerships between donors and institutions may be formed which seek to advance the institution;
5. Annual giving provides a beginning for solicitation for future capital campaigns and for future planned gifts;
6. Trust between the institution and the donor is developed through proper institutional stewardship of gifts, and time that is spent with each individual;
7. Most donors anticipate and expect recognition for their gifts;
8. Involving donors in developing a case statement for support is an easy way of soliciting their future financial support;
9. In any type of fund-raising campaign, 90% of the total amount of money received will come from about 10% of the donors; and
10. Donors give to an institution based on their own needs or interests, and not those that are stated or requested by the institution.

Principles in Action
People Give to People. Of all of the principles of fund raising that exist, perhaps the best known and most frequently referred to is that people give to people. This concept refers to both the actual asking for the gift and the entire cultivation process of preparing a donor for a future gift.

There is no better principle to emphasize the importance of involving faculty members in any and all cultivation and solicitation efforts. Who better than faculty members to "rekindle" the positive feelings that alumni carry of their favorite professors or classes? These beloved professors can also reinforce the concept that alumni "owe" much of what they are today to the college and the faculty members who inspired them.

No matter how long the development or the alumni officer has been on campus, no matter how long a tenure the president has held, in each case, as a student, the alumnus had the most daily contact during the college years with faculty members.

No one else is as able to express passionately or forcefully the needs of a particular department or course of study as well as faculty members, for the faculty must use the equipment, teach, and daily live with the state of their academic disciplines. These faculty best 'paint the picture' of what is needed, and from them, the donor is more likely to listen to the details of the needs or the case for support. Despite what some senior administrators may believe, especially those who have only been on campus for a relatively short period of time, most donors listen more to the view of their former faculty with whom they interacted in their youth.

People want happy experiences that giving to others provides. In their *Seven Faces of Philanthropy*, Prince and File (1994) wrote that most donors have pleasant feelings when giving to an institution that they respect and admire. How is it that faculty and staff could assist in providing donors with these pleasant feelings? Again, the importance of the faculty members' ability to paint a picture or create a vision of what and how potential gifts benefit an institution must be stressed.

The simple thank you of faculty members that can be sent to donors can be a tremendous source of assistance to an institution. This thank you can greatly increase the level of good and pleasant feelings that have been generated from making a gift.

Often, faculty and even board members are frightened or uncomfortable with asking for a contribution. One easy way of providing them with some self-confidence as well as getting them used to being able to solicit a gift is to utilize their talents in making personal telephone calls to thank donors for their gifts.

In completing these thank-you telephone calls, it has been observed that more often than not, while the donor may at first be a little apprehensive about the call, and may be expecting another solicitation for a gift, the donors are frequently pleasantly surprised to hear another person expressing gratitude for the gift. Although research has yet to emphasize this tactic, empirical use, often discussed in professional associations, reinforces the positive influences of faculty assistance in expressing gratitude for financial contributions.

People want to help the institution meet its needs. When alumni are proud of the college they graduated from, when they are proud of the degree that they hold, and when they feel that their education made them what they are today, they are willing to thank the institution either through volunteer work or through a financial contribution.

Faculty members are most able to assist in defining the needs of the institution as well as in defining the mission of the college. Their perceptions of who they are, where they have come from, and where they are going, are the most important to the development office. The faculty are the ones who have instilled a sense of pride in the alumni when they were students, and they demonstrate the mission to alumni and current students. Frequently, it is the faculty and staff members' tenure or desire to remain at the college that influences alumni giving patterns. Lengthy stays at the institution represent satisfaction with the institution to many alumni and demonstrates a loyalty to the mission and needs of the college which encourages donor and alumni loyalty and contributions.

Partnerships between donors and institutions may be formed. Most frequently, donors appreciate the opportunity of forming a partnership with the institution, and donors enjoy feeling that they are part of a "winning team" or a project that will demonstrate success. By sharing in this success, the donors form and feel a partnership and a closeness to the institution.

Perhaps the most logical goal of the professional development officer in higher education is to involve faculty in the very beginning of any fund-raising campaign. Faculty, too, will want to be part of the winning team, and will be able to assist in campaigns both in their preparation and after they have begun.

Relying on faculty and staff allows the development officer to view the campaign from a holistic vantage point. In gaining the input from faculty, the development officer may strategize or more effectively plan to improve the campaign, often by adjusting or enhancing the fund-raising techniques which involve team players such as faculty.

Faculty are excellent in providing additional names of individuals who would be interested in the particular campaign or in developing the specific case for support. They also prove themselves to be invaluable in stating the case for support and in assisting the development officers in refining and honing objectives for raising institutional support.

Annual giving provides a beginning for solicitation for the future. Most fund-raising professionals agree that all giving is arranged in a "donor pyramid." The purpose of the annual fund is to attract the interest of the donor and then to eventually involve the donor in a major or special gift project, followed by a gift to a capital campaign, followed by the pinnacle of all gifts, a planned gift (see Appendix 4).

This pyramid has been the standard for fund-raising practices for at least the past two decades, and continues to influence the majority of development alumni officers. Once a donor has become an annual donor, i.e., once the donor has begun to make a regular annual contribution and has formed an initial loyalty to the institution, it then becomes a matter of cultivation to try to increase this donor's gift and to provide additional mechanisms for providing gifts to the college.

Assuming that the donor is willing to allow some publicity for the gift, this again provides an opportunity to involve faculty in the campaign. If the donor is willing to have a picture appear in a local newspaper, in an alumni newsletter, in a magazine, or in a local television news broadcast, it proves even more effective to include a faculty member and student who benefit from the contribution. This again emphasizes the integrity of the gift, and sends the message that the contribution provides a means of enhancing the educational aspect of the collegiate experience rather than individual or administrative promotion.

Faculty involvement also provides a mechanism for the beginning of cultivation of faculty as potential donors. Although there are always stereotypes that faculty members do not have sufficient financial resources, many faculty members are extremely loyal to their employing institutions. The principle of "if you don't ask, you don't get" holds particularly true for most faculty. Development officers frequently overlook faculty members in developing cultivation programs, thinking that faculty are typically more loyal (in financial terms) to their *alma mater* rather than their employer. Conversely, many faculty may feel honored and pleased to arrange a "living" memorial to themselves and their academic disciplines, perhaps even named after themselves, which would greatly benefit future generations. Just as faculty members can identify potential donors through alumni data bases, they also should be given the opportunity to identify themselves and their colleagues for a current gift or for cultivation for a future gift.

Trust between the institution and the donor is developed through institutional stewardship. Donors who restrict their gifts to a specific department or account are interested in knowing or being shown that the gift really did go to the area requested. The use of faculty to emphasize this receipt, either by a thank you phone call or through informing the donor of the gift's use, does much in assisting the donor to realize that the original contribution has been wisely used. This also demonstrates that the donor has a large degree of control over the contribution and that involvement through giving can make a significant difference.

Even with contributions of unrestricted funds, it is wise to contact donors to inform them of how their gifts have been used. Donors appreciate this personal contact, and frequently will provide additional funding to a project by simply being informed of how their gift has been used, and how additional gifts that will be received may be used in the future.

Most donors anticipate and expect recognition. Most donors do expect some type of recognition for their gifts. In this era of high competition for philanthropic dollars, it seems unusual that there exist some institutions which do not follow the guidelines of acknowledging a gift within seventy-two hours of receipt. Frequently, due to computer problems or a shortage of staff, the processing of gifts can be placed on "the back burner," and as a result, donors do not receive an acknowledgment on a timely basis.

Unless the donor requests anonymity, it is helpful to thank donors as frequently as possible, without adding huge expenditures to the budget. An annual report, as well as quarterly honor roll of donors are always helpful in recognizing donors' generosity and loyalty.

The development office and the administration should determine an amount of a gift in which additional recognition or thanks would be helpful. Naturally, for a minimal contribution, three or four thank you's and a moderate premium would not be cost effective, nor would it be helpful to win future support. However, for more sizable gifts, recognition of this nature coupled with a letter of gratitude from a department chair or faculty member would be most appropriate. Involving the department chair or faculty member in this instance may indeed prove to be more meaningful than from a dean or senior-level administrator, as the faculty recognition demonstrates the power of a contribution at a grass-roots level.

Including faculty members in this acknowledgment process is extremely helpful. Their adding a thank you for a gift to their department or a scholarship fund or their simply writing a "P.S." on a standard acknowledgment letter will do much in encouraging the donor to make future gifts. A phone call, simply to say thank you, also would do much in making the donor feel and realize that the financial aid is truly needed and appreciated by all. This telephone call of acknowledgment is also an excellent teaching and training technique to assist faculty members in overcoming reluctance or apprehension about personally dealing with a contribution, perhaps even laying the ground work for the faculty member to solicit funds. Thanking a donor for a previous gift and not having to ask for a gift is much easier for most individuals. Also, it is a way to relax the caller and acclimate the faculty member in talking about specific dollar amounts, the power of these contributions, and developing an understanding about the procedures and processes used by the institution for fund raising.

Involving donors in developing a case statement is vital to the future. Many development officers conduct a study or a test to determine if the case for support that they have developed will be successful in attracting additional gifts to the college. The case for support is the central theme of any fund-raising campaign, and as a result, it is crucial that as much input as possible is brought into the preparation of the case statement. All too often, development officers rely solely on communication with senior institutional administrators, and neglect the input of instructional and research faculty who have primary responsibility for program quality. The trend in recent years has been token involvement, utilizing nonspecific mailings to faculty asking for their indirect input into "things" that the college or university may "need."

Faculty at the institution will be the most helpful in determining the validity of the request for support, especially if they are willing to financially support it with their own resources. With faculty input, the case may be rewritten several times, until consensus is reached among faculty, academic and academic-support administrators, and development personnel. The intent is to create a vision for the institution which reflects a holistic approach to quality education, and a vision which will elicit support from institutional alumni and friends.

Faculty, as frontline employees, may be able to recall specific instances where students were unable to complete assignments or obtain adequate resources for lack of something specific, such as scholarships, computer technology, study areas, library facilities and resources, etc. That reference or recollection would assist in writing the story or the case, or in presenting that material to the alumni or potential donors. The more input that can be obtained, the better the case for support or the need statement becomes.

Ninety percent of the money comes from 10 percent of the donors. Despite all of the work that is done to involve all of the donors or all of the alumni in making contributions to the college or university, the principle or tenet that has to be remembered is the "90/10" rule: 90 percent of the entire amount of money raised comes from 10 percent of the donors.

Usually, the president, board of trustees, and the development officers will deal with the 10 percent of the wealthy or most generous donors. However, to demonstrate a unified campus as well as assisting in the campus community to feel a sense of accomplishment, it will be necessary to include and work with all donors, whether they are major donors or not. Including faculty and staff members in work with "minor" donors (those who could not contribute a gift in the six figure range, or whatever institutional formula or criteria is used to describe a major donor) is a way of allowing all donors to feel a sense of worth and importance to the institution. Also, it provides the faculty with the opportunity of maintaining contacts with some of their more favorite former students or the more illustrious alumni.

Faculty members looking for assistance with their classes, as far as external speakers to validate what the faculty member is teaching, would be assisted by this particular opportunity to network with the graduates of their institution. Frequently, students need this type of outside or external stimulus (having a successful alumnus returning to the class to talk to students) to be more conscientious as to their studies and to assist them in determining their future career goals.

Donors give to an institution based on their own needs or interests. Again, although this would seem to be a very common sense statement that anyone would understand and grasp, and that anyone would agree with, yet, a number of capital and annual campaigns are established using cases for support that are far too glamorous to encourage a donor to become a participant in the campaign. Cases for support to repair the plumbing fixtures, to comply with the Americans With Disabilities Act, to lay new sewers, and to build parking lots are just a few examples of the lack of foresight or thought that some administrations place in their planning process. There is even a case where a new president wanted to destroy an old building on campus which was not being used, replace it with a parking lot, and cover the current parking lot with an educational excellence center. The motivation for this construction: a demonstration to the community that the college was focused on progress and the arts. As the institution was focused on first-generation, middle-class students, this case was not easily (nor eventually) planned in light of the institution's capabilities or need. The new president, however, believed that he could change the vision of the college early in his tenure, and had no concept that the college, faculty, and key alumni would end up in turmoil over his grand ideas.

The key to planning effective fund raising is to garner alumni and potential donor support, and develop consensus on campus between those constituents and campus constituents, particularly faculty and students. Faculty members, if they are indeed responsible for institutional prestige (through research, teaching, service, and preparing future alumni), must be involved in communicating with the potential donors to find a common set of needs. In this scenario, the development office becomes a fulcrum in which different power centers are brought to collaboration.

Involving Faculty in Development

Faculty members need to be involved in the fund-raising process. This is true, as the dollars raised will usually most influence the faculty, either through scholarships that are offered to attract better or more qualified students, or through improvements that are for the betterment of their departments.

Some development officers may claim that there are some negatives associated with including faculty in the identification and solicitation of donors. They feel that faculty may unduly influence donors so that they are able to obtain items that they personally want, or are able to influence donors to support their individual cases for support. Many development office personnel also claim that faculty are slow to respond, lack organization to follow in garnering involvement, and place individual needs above institutional needs.

Many institutions also follow the custom of having students who are receiving scholarships or financial aid write to donors to thank them for the financial assistance. Most frequently, the development office will monitor the letter writing to first make sure that it is grammatically correct and to make certain the student or recipient does not ask the donor for additional financial assistance after college, or for other nonacademic needs.

Although there are some gauges or tests that exist that can be used to identify the best individuals to solicit potential donors for contributions, frequently it will be necessary for the development officers to identify the best faculty members for involvement. Some may volunteer who actually will prove to be a detriment to the college and its programs. The most common form of soliciting faculty involvement is through traditional governance mechanisms, such as asking a college dean for faculty members who might be involved. This top-down identification, however, may often prove to be both discouraging for faculty who recognize the power of involvement in fund raising, and frustrating for those working to establish clear lines of faculty involvement through a senate or similar forum.

Faculty can play an important role in institutional fund raising, but this role is one which must be bartered among faculty and administrative groups. There are real benefits to involving faculty in fund raising, and faculty must learn to accept this type of behavior if they intend to benefit from it. Current barriers concerning the involvement of faculty in resource allocation tend to be perceptual—on both the part of faculty who may resent being asked to do this and administrators who may see faculty unfit for this type of service. Efforts to maximize institutional effectiveness, then, must be educational in nature to begin with, but must also be visionary and mutually beneficial.

For Discussion
1. Is there a way of terminating a faculty volunteer who is proving to be a detriment to the college and its advancement program?
2. Should faculty members be allowed to work with alumni and donors only after they have made their own financial contribution?
3. What process needs to be in place to include faculty members in the long-range development plan or strategic planning process of the institutional advancement office?
4. At what point should donors be stopped from restricting their gifts to certain departments or colleges, rather than giving unrestricted gifts which may be used where the need is greatest?

5. Will alumni respond better to solicitations by department, class year, or other academic unit? Based on this answer, is there a method for measuring the effectiveness of faculty involvement?

Section 3

Making Use of the Shared Governance Process

Chapter 6
Faculty Involvement in Evaluating Institutional Effectiveness and Planning
by Thomas F. McCormack and Exir Brennen

Anyone of slight acquaintance with higher education is aware of the fulsome and happy period following World War II, when funding was ever expanding, and colleges and universities were the bright stars ascending. Then, shock tremors set in, as a result of the economic recession of 1974-1975, with its concomitant declines in public funding of higher education. A few institutions began to retrench, developing strategies for coping with cutbacks. Kaufman (1971), Glenny (1976), Levine (1978) and others have begun to warn all of higher education that attempting to resist decline would be risky, and that the only viable response would be adaptation. Cyert (1978), predicting a period of decline in higher education funding, called for effective strategic planning, and for institutions to find an equilibrium position at some smaller size. At the time of Cyerts' writing, excellence in higher education was "usually bought through surplus funds, not from priority setting and reallocation" (p. 90). Mingle (1981) was one of many to suggest a wide variety of tools, strategies, and solutions for consideration by faculty groups and other institutional constituencies confronted with harsh planning realities. Effectiveness did not appear thematic in the strategies; perhaps "lip service" to standards and practices assisted in the germination of the ensuing current educational environment that yields today's product. To some in education, economic necessity is the driving force of change, because as never before, survival is now at stake.

Is There A Need to Change?

Public Call for Accountability

In times of retrenchment and reduction, there is a sense of urgency about the effectiveness and responsiveness of most state government systems. As the decade of the 1980s passed, conditions grew more acute, and currently, as the late 1990s approach the millennium, another thunderous realization is occurring: no longer will the public accept the notion that, given the returns on investment, American higher education is cheap (Levine, 1997). Thorny perceptions persist related to how much (money) is enough and what is a good school (quality of product)? All education is being held accountable for its returns to the public. The system must produce graduates who are fit for the marketplace, and do it with far fewer resources. Most difficult of all, this new public demand means that each institution must ultimately substantiate its own reason for existence. Public concerns over large tuition increases, the failure of higher education to recruit and graduate significant numbers of minority students, scandals concerning the academic performance of athletes, large student loan defaults, cost overruns in the overhead charges for federal research grants, and campus crime have undermined confidence in American higher education. As a result of these concerns, a majority of states have enacted legislation requiring increased assessment of student learning (Wolff & Harris, 1994).

Numerous national reports and a joint Congressional hearing on the need to reform higher education have jarred the higher education community. Various higher education associations have helped to shape responses to these pressures, as have the growing literature and research on assessment. These facts notwithstanding, faculty attention and genuine commitment to assessment have been difficult, if not impossible to attain in many institutions. Many faculty perceive the assessment of outcomes as a response to demonstrate the value of the college experience to those external to the institution who may or may not have the discriminating ability to value the process as well as the product.

Accrediting Agencies' Role

In 1978, two regional accrediting agencies for higher education, the North Central Association and the Southern Association of Colleges and Schools, already strong advocates for self-evaluation, began promulgating policies for outcome assessment (Young, 1981). While accreditation had always functioned as an evaluation and assessment process, this type of assessment was unfamiliar to most institutions, especially as it related to the real effectiveness of an institution. Accreditation traditionally had focused on resource inputs, but as the Southern Association of Colleges and Schools' Commission on Colleges reported, the addition of this criterion "represents an expansion of the process to emphasize the results of education and to focus on the extent to which the institution uses assessment information to...make essential improvements and to plan for the future" (SACS, 1996, p. iii).

Assessment of outcomes thus had a much broader connotation. The entire institution must be assessed in terms of how well it has precisely met its goals. Accrediting agencies are referring to this as "institutionalizing" the process (SACS, 1996). Reluctant or not, faculty cannot escape involvement. Dr. Barbara Curry, in *Instituting Enduring Innovations: Achieving Continuity of Change in Higher Education* (1992) described institutionalization as reflected in multiple concrete ways throughout an organization, i.e., something is institutionalized when it is part of a legitimate and ongoing practice, infused with value and supported by all aspects of a system. Effectiveness assessment may be seen by faculty as a threat, the "long arm of some superordinate body" placing its ugly hands on the faculty's sacred domain (Ratcliff, 1989). Others see assessment as an end in itself, to be used in making statements about accountability to the public. However assessment may be viewed, and reluctant or not, faculty cannot escape involvement.

Federal and State Impetus

Policy makers are demanding greater accountability in how their tax dollars are spent, and they are increasingly asserting that these dollars are being misspent. Even a U. S. Congressional committee recently condemned higher education institutions for their lack of responsiveness to the needs of college students (Education Commission of the States, 1992). A number of national reports by higher education professional organizations have supported this conclusion (Association of American Colleges, 1985).

In the January 10, 1997 issue of *The Chronicle of Higher Education*, thirty states were reported as expecting "chilly responses" from state funding agencies. One state agency referred to its legislative request as "pie-in-the-sky." None of these states expected anything more than level or decreased funding for higher education. Concomitantly, institutions were being asked to do more about controlling colleges costs to students and the taxpayers. Such a mandate reflected not just a conservative tone, but a totally different, cost-centered approach to education funding.

Faculty Tradition and Ambition

An image of the American professoriate as a group unable to comprehend the world around them is again in ascendance. But it no longer refers to the kind of respectable bemusement that once characterized American attitudes toward collegiate faculty. There is, instead, a sense that the professor belongs to a privileged class largely out of touch with the tough realities of the 1990s (Zemsky, 1996). Generously-paid professors do very little teaching, research takes priority over teaching, and undergraduate students suffer in the process by paying more while their educational needs are neglected (Education Commission of the States, 1992).

Higher education has long prided itself on its uncoupled nature, the absence of need for any connectedness. Colleges and universities are the marketplaces of free inquiry, and as such, they ostensibly produce critical thinkers, self-motivated, and independent of any kind of mold imposed externally. Faculty have cherished the notion that they are not obliged to compete for a market (Brubacher, 1988). In other words, higher education has not heretofore been forced to describe its "product," or graduate, as would be necessary to satisfy a paying public. Even the curricula that makes up degree programs to produce the graduate are fragmented such that it is difficult to find coherence and structure (Association of American Colleges, 1985).

Some recent research has indicated that faculty are responding to external incentives, and that the research model which was imposed upon faculty by the need to generate external money is changing (National Center for Educational Statistics, 1996). Ernest Boyer called for a more inclusive view of what it means to be a scholar, and that the scholarship of teaching be given significant weight in productivity analyses (Boyer, 1990). Zemsky (1996) insisted that faculty, far from being oblivious to the world around them, are overwhelmed and that they are reacting in defense. As smart people, the faculty have simply become more adept at denial, because they are unsure of what business they are in. When new technologies and new demands are introduced, denial is well-honed: business people have no perspective for defining what a college graduate should be; technology is just a quick-fix for lazy students; and, higher education's monopoly over the college degree is unassailable, according to traditionalists.

Regardless, Wagner and Kemmerer (1985) argued that most professors know the rules for success in their profession. As smart people, a new generation of faculty are likely to be practical in outlook, more ambitious, and more likely to respond positively to questions such as "What are the citizens of this state receiving for their investment in higher education?" And many senior faculty are willing to teach more, and to respond appropriately to a different student culture. A college education is still seen by the public as the way to improve one's economic opportunities, and the teaching role involved in preparing students for job markets is apparent to faculty who may have also borne a substantial portion of their own education. In effect, by way of example and precept, they are willing to demonstrate that the products of their efforts, the graduates, can be successfully marketed. In the practical sense, the assessment of outcomes and institutional effectiveness is a new dimension of the professoriate's workload.

Changing from Within

Measuring Effectiveness as Accountability

The fact that at most campuses, the greatest rewards are given for research which is often in esoteric areas and published in sparsely circulated journals the public and state legislators do not find meritorious, or that they even know about. Instead, the public focus is on college graduates who can get jobs, education equal to tuition, and solutions to economic concerns, the work force, and changing society (Layzell, Lovell, & Gill, 1996). But professors know this, even without constant reminders by state and federal agencies.

Townsend, Newell, and Wiese (1992) have described two paradigms for strategic management of colleges and universities, to make them distinctive (paraphrase "responsive") to the critics and funding sources in the current milieu, and to increase the probability of institutional survival during times of intense competition. These are the adaptive model, which regards organizations as living organisms with rationally defined, achievable goals, and the interpretive model which emphasizes individual involvement in networks, wherein the leaders weave individual needs into a culture. The authors illustrated the two paradigms with examples of distinctive institutions across the U. S. In both models, the starting point for the distinctive institution must be a unifying vision representing members' values, and "each model calls for innovation, entrepreneurship, and educational revolution" (p. 57). In each successful case, the faculty, including the most tradition-bound, have committed to change, and in some cases were instigators for the entire institution. Where faculty have captured or created some sense of community and mutual understanding of crises, they act. Seymour (1988) articulated the belief of planners such as Cyert and Kaufman, among others, by stating that planning and decision-making on campuses work best with a high level of faculty involvement and a clear understanding of priorities. However, Seymour cautioned, there will be no planning at all without discipline imposed upon an organization from a central source. Leadership affects faculty responsiveness.

Considering the impact of the current crisis in funding, leadership will do well to communicate its expectations for involvement in decision-making to the faculty, and faculty leaders will in turn serve themselves and colleagues when they provide support rather than deny circumstances. Thomas Kuhn, in *The Structure of Scientific Revolutions*, conveyed an example of how paradigms limit people

> An investigator who hoped to learn something about what scientists took the atomic theory to be asked a distinguished physicist an eminent chemist whether a single atom of helium was or was not a molecule. Both answered without hesitation, but their answers were not the same. For the chemist the atom of helium was a molecule because it displayed no particular spectrum. For the physicist, on the other hand, the helium atom was not a molecule because it displayed no molecular spectrum. Presumably both men were talking of the same particle, but they were viewing it through their own research, training and practice. (1970, p. 50)

As long as faculty and administrators can understand diversity in thinking, they can change.

The accreditation agencies' requirements for measurements of institutional effectiveness have afforded leadership a well focused opportunity to call upon faculty as agents to predicate needed changes based on these measurements. Such measurements must profile the entire operations of an institution, including budget implementation. Very few faculty members, when given the true opportunity, will ignore the budget, even when it may indicate constraints. The measurement of student learning outcomes as a part of institutional effectiveness, once the only domain of the faculty, is a responsibility which all must share. In reality, the outcomes measurement movement is an exciting opportunity for faculty to affect the direction of the institution.

To Do the Impossible

Protective fences have almost always been built between college fiscal officers and faculty. Administrators do not think the faculty capable of understanding anything numerical, while faculty believe all fiscal officers to be prevaricators. Hence, all of the tomes proclaiming that no true linkages can or do exist between academic planning and budgeting (Collier, 1988).

The AAUP *Statement on Government of Colleges and Universities* contained the provision that budgeting is central to the educational function of the faculty (American Association of University Professors, 1966). The statement termed this a responsibility of the faculty. Attendant to this responsibility, according to AAUP, was the need for the broadest possible exchange of information and opinion among the components of the college or university.

The National Association of College and University Business Officers, the gate keepers to budget and finance in higher education, warned that a "participatory approach to strategic decision-making may be counterproductive precisely because it is managed by those with a stake in the outcome" (NACUBO, 1992, p. 31). However, even this authority has seen faculty and the chief academic officer as key players in decision formation; even implementation.

A more auspicious moment for faculty demonstration of its prudence and wisdom has never existed than the opportunity which now exists. Given that they have been charged with living in luxury without the necessity for performance, with an uncaring attitude toward its chief clients (students), and with ignoring public demands, the professoriate can seek and assume responsibility for stewardship of the public resources it has been given. This is not to say that all faculty must learn to be accountants. In fact, great care must be taken to find the correct balance between efficiency and effectiveness, versus the breadth and length of vision necessary to healthy planning.

Only **selected** improvements and changes can be managed in light of budget crises and reductions. The annualized planning processes at some colleges and universities present a panorama of choices among programs, building, practices, policies and procedures for review and establishment of priorities among all the choices.

Decision makers in faculty committees in many cases have all the data they need to make difficult choices which result in some of the needed improvements. A key to practice is mutually rating areas for improvement, and suggesting calendars for action. All parties will never be satisfied, but the process of informing and mutually sharing a better understanding of crises and all problem areas can assist the implementation process.

Faculty can progress beyond the notion that this is merely a political process. In spite of rumor and innuendo, college decision makers have real cases of crisis to present. Planning processes at some institutions have already generated "information communities," but all constituencies must accept that products of the planning process are not simply paper.

Jones and Lovell (1993) suggested that faculty as human resources are institutional assets, and should be viewed as a long-term institutional investment to be developed and maintained. Institutional managers who embrace this perspective must contemplate questions of what is necessary to maintain this asset, which involves a determination of whether the prospective asset can contribute to the existing environment (Layzell, Lovell, & Gill, 1996). Concomitantly, then, the faculty will disengage from its separate existence, and contemplate its contribution, even if this means perceived sacrifice. Tying faculty activities and responsibilities to the achievement of state and public needs requires a significant shift in the way everyone on campus thinks about higher education. Only with this shift can faculty and higher education regain the public's support and confidence. A change in academic culture must occur, from an orientation to state rather than discipline needs, and a change in campus approach to faculty development and incentives (Layzell, Lovell, & Gill, 1996). In a sense, institutions must return to the service orientations, such as those originally identified as part of the Morrill legislation in the 1860s.

Townsend, Novell, and Wiese (1994) have defined the distinctive institution as the result of a social and professional contract among faculty and institutional professionals, unified on a primary purpose. Distinctiveness, according to these authors, should aid decision-making, even regarding fiscal management. Having a guiding vision could cause faculty to assist in deleting programs, or to consolidate and redefine programmatic areas in times of financial exigency. Such decisions are facile when programs are evaluated in terms of true centrality to mission. At the state level, allocating resources is also easier when they are distributed according to distinctiveness (Morgan & Newell, 1981).

Strohm (1980) was concerned that the "soft" retrenchment that many faculty had experienced would make "hard" retrenchment much more difficult. For Strohm, the catalyst for getting faculty to participate in hard decisions was financial exigency. Strohm suggested a distinctive strategy for faculty, which was to pre-plan careful guidelines to cover states of retrenchment under exigency, but if a bona fide exigency occurred, the plan should provide that faculty accept responsibility for developing criteria for necessary termination and program truncations. Few, if any, faculty groups have implemented such a distinctive strategy.

Creating Distinctiveness

Leaders who aspire to distinctiveness "...must clearly state the unifying value(s) around which individuals and institutions will rally" (Townsend, Newell, & Wiese, 1992, p. 61-62). Some colleges have focused on new program areas and new clienteles, others have narrowed or expanded mission and goal statements, while some have unified under a theme such as becoming the "best buy for the money." Georgia State University, for example, set out to be the latter, as well as to become the most accessible institution with the most flexible scheduling. GSU successfully and quickly created distinctiveness, and has grown more than any other institution in Georgia (Hossley & Bean, 1990). Elmhurst College established a model for others by developing degree programs aimed solely at working adults and has become a model for collaborative learning (Goodsell, 1992). All distinctive institutions have assumed the inevitable risks involved with developing a particular niche.

In an era of severe fiscal constraints and financial uncertainty, Alabama A&M University's leadership in the fall of 1996 began unifying faculty under the theme of a "new attitude." This new attitude was promulgated through a catharsis which involved faculty in a minute examination of all academic programs, across the institution, and in detailed analyses of the direct costs of these programs. The end results of the process included program deletion and peer review for purposes of reducing faculty numbers. The new attitude which emerged was that a sleepy, sprawling land grant institution could, in a relatively short time, completely reorient staff and faculty, and actually define improved quality in terms of sleekness, efficiency, and effectiveness.

Once an institution has realized its distinctiveness, it inevitably is emulated. It may be that the most substantive result of involving faculty in the development of distinctiveness, however, is that the traditionally, and often carefully preserved gap between administrators and faculty is bridged. Townsend and colleagues (1992) called for "groundbreakers" to plant seeds of innovation and distinctiveness so that higher education will have new paths; it is now time for faculty to assume this role.

Faculty involvement must become a cornerstone of change for higher education to maintain its monopoly on the collegiate experience. Through authentic, meaningful and rational decision-making, faculty can play an important role in defining how institutions confront new challenges. This involvement, to be effective, must grow from institutional efforts to identify and forecast who they are and where they want to be. Planning, as a vital part of higher education's future, must incorporate both faculty, administrators, off-campus constituents, students, alumni, and staff, and for each of these to play their individual roles effectively, institutional resources must similarly become part of the common conversation about the future of higher learning.

For Discussion

1. To what extent should faculty be involved in budgeting? What types of control and responsibility should accompany this involvement, and what are the requirements for training faculty to deal with budgets?
2. How is institutional effectiveness defined? How are faculty and administrators to be involved in measuring this effectiveness? With which criteria is it most appropriate for faculty to be involved?
3. Define representativeness. Does participation equate with, or become equated with representativeness? How

should representativeness be structured in discussing the effectiveness of a faculty governance unit?
4. What is the potential impact of non-responsiveness on the part of faculty? From administrative, trustee, and faculty perspectives, how do institutions respond to non-responsiveness?
5. How is and how should faculty involvement be made accountable?

Chapter 7
Putting it all Together: Effective Faculty Governance
by Kathleen Randall and Michael T. Miller,
University of Alabama

Although inclusive governance structures are considered to be preferable in academic communities, they are in fact quite difficult to develop and maintain. The commitment of upper level administrators to the advantages of shared governance models can quickly erode when faced with complex and challenging issues related to actual practice. The implementation of various models designed to empower faculty in the institutional decision-making process can lead to faculty suspicion or apathy rather than enthusiasm on the part of academia. With this in mind, what is an effective strategy? Is the effort to establish a trusting, shared partnership worth the journey? What obstacles to shared authority remain on the horizon?

Questions such as these are vital to institution-wide acceptance of broad-based inclusive decision-making, and only an institutional-wide approach to shared governance can produce the potential key benefits and results. The approach to be taken, however, requires effort of both administrators and faculty, and must be respectful and encouraging of staff involvement as well. True involvement means that power must be shared by all parties involved, and this give and take must be done with trust, mutual respect, and constant, open communication. Most campuses have the infrastructure necessary to create shared governing communities, yet few are anxious to experiment with bold new and different techniques in decision-making.

The Involved Faculty

Models of faculty involvement include both the formal mechanisms, such as faculty senates and councils, and the less formal and often more influential processes of involvement, including standing and special committees as well as individual faculty efforts. The effectiveness of any form of faculty involvement is reliant on the ability of the faculty to express, intelligibly, articulately, convincingly, and rationally, the collective belief of the faculty body. This requires the faculty to be purposive in their deliberations, but also requires respect, trust, and adherence on the part of the administrators.

Advantages to faculty governance can be real and meaningful for a campus; however, in order to achieve these advantages, both faculty and administrators must be prepared to make concessions. The primary responsibility for the actualization of faculty ownership and empowerment lies with administrators at the dean's level and higher. Department heads and chairs define the parameters for involvement and help to establish the accepted norms for the quantity of involvement. But it is the dean, provost, president, and others within this realm who have the power to accept, reject, or broadly value the input of faculty. Administrators are not required to accept faculty decisions, but even the appearance of consideration of faculty effort is a necessity as a symbol of valuing faculty work.

Another, and often controversial area for the encouragement of participation is through the creation and maintenance of a reward structure which places some quantifiable value on participation. From one perspective, this may be the consideration of merit or tenure and promotion criteria. On another level, this recognition may take the form of release time from teaching to hold a leadership position, secretarial or institutional research support, or inclusion of faculty leaders in the senior administrative staff meetings.

Assessing Inclusive Decision Making

Several conditions affect the development of true teamwork (Bensimon & Neumann, 1993). First, the president must feel comfortable with a more inclusive, and perhaps, more egalitarian system. "This partnership is likely to involve listening to voices that have not traditionally been at the center of the decision process rather than favoring convention (and dominant) views" (p. 51). Clearly, upper level management needs to be committed to a more open setting. This might translate into the ability to withstand resistance from other administrators who view faculty as more appropriately involved in matters related to scholarship or narrowly defined policies related to academic progress alone.

Research has indicated that college presidents often perceive that they are inclusive, while the planning and decision-making models of the campus are perceived by faculty to be withdrawn and aloof. Continuous communication and renewal of commitment to these principles are key factors to ongoing success. Regular methods for reviewing the governance model's effectiveness might be in place to ascertain whether differing opinions are listened to or discounted. Otherwise, presidents and other campus administrative leaders can mislead even themselves into believing an inclusive environment has been put into place when other members of the academic community believe something quite to the contrary (Birnbaum, 1991).

Perhaps the avenues least resistant to ongoing direct faculty involvement are those matters of concern to the academic standards of the institution. Governing boards and provosts are likely to find it quite logical to seek faculty guidance on such decisions as admissions standards, curricular offerings, and graduation requirements. The degree of faculty authority in these issues, of course, varies according to the institutions leadership (Brubacher, 1988).

One of the more difficult areas for assessing shared governance relates to the quality of faculty effort. Several research based projects have described participation in terms of quantity, yet few efforts have been directed at the quality of faculty input into decision-making. Although this may be difficult to measure, social scientists such as Glendon Shubert have worked to profile effectiveness in public, inclusive decision-making environments. For example, Shubert, although mostly dealing with issues of chronological and relative age in political behavior, worked to identify decision-making in municipal governments. He held the belief that participation is no guarantee of quality decision-making, and that the true test of an inclusive environment lies in the ability of decisions to be accepted and implemented, even if those decisions upset or unsettle administrators who would prefer alternatives.

Additionally, senior faculty who have endured several terms and styles of administrative leadership need to challenge their own biases or tendencies not to trust new models as genuinely open. The development of true teamwork must be built on trust that is both mutually earned and maintained. Once these models are in place, the lack of trust is likely to subside.

Evidence of eroding commitment to shared governance may be indicated by:

1. Changes in communication patterns, such as a lack of written response to faculty committee and standing committee annual reports;

2. Decisions made in haste without adequate opportunity for faculty dialog;

3. Publications and or speeches seeming to be more interested in positive "spin" rather than honest appraisal of the campus's strengths and weaknesses;

4. Deterioration of relaxed, more personal interaction between faculty and staff leadership;

5. Passivity or frustration among the faculty leaders in terms of feeling there is not much benefit in objecting to a campus plan or policy under review;

6. Attrition problems among the faculty senate or other body designed to ascertain faculty opinion on campus matters.

7. Withdrawal of faculty back into their more isolated departmental settings.

Whether the issue at hand is one pertaining to athletics, student affairs, or academic policy, campus leaders should invite input and openly receive it. This may often involve the learning of new ways for communication for administrations. The decisions which come as a result of more open communication should receive more universal support, and therefore, lead to a shared vision for the campus.

Clearly, the challenge is in making the process work. Many designs and models have been developed for effective institutional governance. The ability of the leaders to nurture and maintain trust and open communication may rest more with the individual than any formula. As many have written, administration is in itself an art when properly conducted.

Recommendations for successful implementation of revitalizing shared governance models are by their very nature both predictable and elusive. A spirit of collegiality is easier to espouse than to actually accomplish. Even if the majority of key players endorse the underlying principles of inclusiveness, dissension is likely to become evident as difficult decisions are reached.

For Administrators

The management style of campus leaders is more successful when based on trust and openness with the faculty. Faculty citizenship should be encouraged and supported.

New mechanisms for increased communication must be considered and developed to meet the distinctive mission and dynamics particular to the campus.

Citizenship should be rewarded through tenure review and new recognition programs that demonstrate the administration's sincere emphasis on the value of faculty service. The importance of citizenship for the campus must be reiterated to academic deans and viewed as worthwhile. The list below provides suggestions for improved communication and encouragement of active faculty participation in the institution's governance model.

Administrative Strategies for Encouraging Communication and Citizenship

These recommendations are drawn largely from the expertise of the professionals who have contributed the previous chapters. With no exact science to draw upon, and based largely on observations, willingness, and caring attitudes of effective practitioners, these strategies are offered for both discussion, use, and experimentation. The ultimate goal remains: how can faculty involvement help create a more effective college operating environment?

- Recognize exemplary faculty of all ranks who model appropriate citizenship while maintaining scholarship as first priority.

- Seek faculty advice and input on policies and plans as they are being developed rather than in final form.

- Increase personal availability for frank discussions through such informal gatherings as town hall meetings and department head coffees.

- Establish a mentoring program matching new faculty with collegial senior faculty who successfully model the balance between publishing, teaching, and service.

Making Use of the Shared Governance Process   137

- Utilize technology for increased communication such as a shared vision, faculty governing body minutes, a 'chat page' for timely campus issues, and divisional goals on the institution's website.

- Continually reiterate that higher education communities must value each opinion no matter how contradictory or varied.

- Clarify for new faculty their roles in terms of participation in academic decision-making and service to the academic community.

- Provide facilitation training to committee chairpersons in order to welcome input and solicit opinions from various campus constituencies

    Upper level administrators set the tone for the campus by encouraging open participation at all levels. To accomplish this, they generally find a management philosophy and style that is genuinely participative and empowering of others to be most effective. Other staff in the central administration should assist in recognizing and emphasizing faculty citizenship on a continual basis. Although it may be difficult to maintain an adequate level of emphasis for the shared governance process to function appropriately, often the attempt to be participative will yield fruitful results.

Recognition Strategies for Enhancing a Shared Governance System

    Upper level administrators should contribute to the effective operations of a shared governance system by making deliberate efforts to emphasize its importance. The list below provides specific actions to encourage shared authority and recognize its successful implementation.

- Host midyear progress review sessions for internal

standing committees and respond to all year end reports and strategies submitted in writing.

- Encourage regular review of administration and faculty handbooks.

- Avoid the temptation of becoming isolated from the dynamics of the campus by meeting primarily with central staff and others in subordinate, loyal positions.

- Be careful not to endorse every faculty issue to such a degree that the administrator's open door policy undermines the authority of deans and department heads as well as collegiality at all levels.

- Adequately fund faculty development and support excellent faculty service in the governance processes with a high profile in campus publications.

- Support to the greatest extent possible those departments that have demonstrated effectiveness and collegiality through service to the academic community.

- Empower advisory mechanisms and task forces with the charge of implementing their recommended strategies.

Supporting an environment of excellence in teaching, research, and service can be a slow paced construction. Encouraging a reward system based on three types of performance can be difficult, particularly when directives are brought about by external bodies, such as boards of trustees, new presidents or chancellors hired with a particular vision, and even in changes in categorical allocations to direct institutional activities. Shared decision-making similarly does not evolve simply because most parties believe it to be the desirable model of governance; it can only become reality with considerable consistent effort, and the ability to frankly challenge other members of the community without fear of reprisal or, perhaps worse, fear of being marginalized.

For Faculty

The preceding seven chapters outline a variety of techniques and methods for increasing the ability of faculty to be involved in institutional decision-making. This involvement ranges from acquiring new knowledge and processing available research to the political aspect of brokering deals for the welfare of the campus. Ellsworth (1997) argued that the key to making effective changes is in the learning process and the assumptions of the organization to outline and define the kinds of learning necessary for growth. If this holds true for higher education as well as the private sector, then the primary focus of faculty governance leaders needs to be in defining how governance units frame their work and the "learning" necessary to function effectively.

Faculty have the abilities to participate on an intellectual level with campus governance, however the structural paradigm of unit must evolve more fully. Although each campus environment will differ, the preceding chapters provide a framework for effectiveness based on five key elements.

1. Responsibility

Faculty, and particularly faculty governance units, must accept responsibility in pursuing shared governance. One of the primary complaints about co-governance is the inability of the governance unit to respond quickly and effectively to decisions which must be made in a timely fashion. Monthly meetings of faculty units and related subcommittees do not lend themselves to rapid response. Relying on intuition or situational data does not provide support for a governance unit's success. Effective, responsible governance depends on the willingness of faculty to give up valuable time to pursue and network with individuals in positions to gather data to make meaningful decisions. Collaboration with institutional research and supporting offices can only strengthen the ability of the unit to make meaningful, substantive decisions and recommendations based on logical and sound rationale. Success will be determined by the ability of the unit to respond and take responsibility for these decisions.

2. Democratic Ideals

The governance concept is based generally on the constructs of representative democracy, and as such, faculty must be willing to share issues and concerns with colleagues not directly involved. Participation must be for the good of the institution, and individual academic differences and personal preferences must at times be put aside to create a positive environment. Those elected or appointed to governance units must actively share information related to critical decisions to be made and policies to be developed. These representatives must then be willing to listen and respond to those they represent. Although representation at many institutions is seen as an intrusion on an individual's time, it is a position which demands respect and attention among colleagues. Only through voicing concerns and ascertaining constituents' views can representatives truly work to make a more collegial and effective institution.

3. Integrity

The effectiveness of a faculty governance unit is strongly related to integrity of both the individual faculty members and the group as a whole. The unit must be willing to respond to issues handed "down" from senior administrators, but must also be willing to challenge and fight these administrators on issues of importance to the institution if necessary. As those exposed daily to the needs and concerns of students, faculty must expand their role in working for the good of the institution, representing concerns to the administration. Additionally, as college presidents and provosts become increasingly concerned with the external world of alumni donors, board members, the press, and state legislators, faculty must work to retain the academic integrity of the institution. At times this means publicly challenging and confronting presidents and vice presidents, and at times, supporting unpopular decisions for the benefit of the academic climate of the campus. Those holding the highest positions within the governance units should be particularly aware of the temptation of becoming "puppet governments" of the administration, but similarly must understand that their roles are not inherently adversarial.

4. Role Definition

Much of the ambiguity of the intent and function of a faculty governance unit comes from the inability to define what is and what is not the purview of the unit. Although faculty have no legal right to involvement, each governance unit administration must work to define what they are entitled to have domain over, and what respect or response to their concerns will be given by administrators. Faculty leaders often assume a presidency or chair position of a governance unit basing their expectations on the previous year or predecessor's management style. These individuals in particular must take the opportunity to define the role of the governance unit and its leaders early, negotiating support for these definitions with those who grant the unit power. This may be as simple as a meeting with the campus president or provost, and may be as complex as polling faculty over what they see as their academic rights in governance. Once this power is granted or assumed, the unit has a responsibility to protect and utilize this power.

5. Willingness to Lead

Perhaps the biggest obstacle to effective faculty co-governance, and a theme addressed consistently throughout each chapter, is the willingness of faculty to take on the responsibility for providing the leadership for the institution. Historically, faculty have held this power in appointing individuals from among their own ranks to serve as senior administrators, a trend which is increasingly being reversed as presidents, chancellors, and provosts are hired to appease external constituencies and boards of trustees or directors. Faculty have an opportunity to challenge or support these administrators, although real opposition tends to be limited to a few segmented issues and token roles on search committees. The AAUP has done an outstanding job in working to support faculty groups with grievances, but relying on external consultants or agencies to mediate differences is often a last resort that all but dooms the peaceful coexistence of faculty and administration. The temptation is repeatedly to do as was done before; for institutional growth, real faculty ownership, and a sense of community for the good of all, faculty must be willing to take key leadership positions in defining what will be done on their campuses and must be willing to accept criticism for these actions. Co-governance can be an effective and important issue on any campus, but only if faculty are willing to take the leadership role and restore it to the faculty ranks.

Envisioning the Future of Involved Governance

Business practices and corporate models are likely to continue evolving, and as a result, will continue to influence the governance models of higher education. From quality circles to TQM, the business formulas for decision making and policy development tend to be factors in the collegiate environment.

As fiscal management of institutions becomes more accountable to public scrutiny, it is likely that faculty will be invited to participate in advocacy with legislators regarding the financial needs of their home campuses. With this in mind, it is probable that central administrative leaders will rely more heavily on an open communication style in order to facilitate and nurture faculty support. Faculty senates or councils often speak openly regarding policies under consideration. It is far more reasonable to include them in governing procedures and seek input before a policy goes into effect rather than after the fact. For this reason, many college leaders are redefining their management style to be more inclusive.

While the less hierarchical models are generally considered to be more effective, it must be noted that faculty time and workload considerations will arise. Service and academic citizenship might gain more recognition. Skills for faculty effectiveness in an inclusive management team will need to be developed. Examples include strategic planning and conflict resolution for leaders of quality circles or task forces. Rather than serving in a more polite, collegial environment, it is likely that empowered faculty representatives will find themselves struggling along with administrators with such difficult decisions as downsizing and financial planning.

Skills for oral communication as well as organizational ability will continue to be necessary for effective teamwork. Administrators might need to be retrained to operate in a less hierarchical fashion, and faculty may be in need of training on topics such as constituent demand responsiveness, social economics, and planning. As has been true with corporate leaders, upper level administrators might benefit from observing colleagues from other campuses who successfully operate in a more inclusive environment.

The college campus of the future may also find the student affairs function increasingly a part of the academic affairs enterprise, a trend foreshadowed by the current growth and strengthening of the provost position. In this environment, student affairs professionals may see their role in inviting faculty input to be stressed and made easier. Conversely, the de-emphasis of student affairs may prove problematic in viewing the holistic development of students outside of an academic environment.

For the future of faculty involvement in governance, state coordinating bodies and legislatures which prove to be ineffective in outlining a realistic master plan for their states' institutions may find a growth of organized labor. As institutions and their leaders struggle to define workload, raises, working environment, evaluation strategies and the like, faculty may grow dissatisfied and demand accountability from administrators. Union activity, such as the strikes by college faculty in the mid-1990s, illustrates an effective trend in negotiating compensation. Faculty may find the return on the union investment to be great, with the sacrifice coming at the hands of the autonomy which has for so long been the hallmark of the academic enterprise.

As colleges look to cut costs and engage in more efficient fiscal management, out-sourcing will become even more commonplace. This attention focuses on searching for the best fiscal deal for the institution, and potentially relegates academic integrity to a secondary issue. This type of behavior will further the divide between administrators and faculty, and conflict which may already be tense will be worsened.

Technology may also be a factor which works to redefine how faculty work in the college setting. Although technology primarily has focused on delivery methods and learning enhancement, there are concerns about what role technology will play in the need for faculty. Videotaped or online courses require different demands on faculty, and while learning to deal with these new demands can take time away from involvement, the technology itself may work to replace the faculty member.

Throughout this chapter, a series of strategies and thoughts are offered on the state and future of involving faculty in institutional governance. The underlying theme is that faculty have to want to be involved, and administrators have to learn how to utilize faculty input. The future for shared authority lies in a common understanding of expectations and two-way communication which respects individual thinking and behavior. Trends and mechanisms to date have not developed to a state of true understanding, but the seeds for growth, present in such activities as faculty task forces and in faculty senates, represents hope for a future of shared authority which seeks to benefit the learning and growth of the college student.

For Discussion

1. What is the future of different types of institutions, including community and technical colleges, liberal arts colleges, teaching and research universities? What are the primary challenges they will face in the future? What leadership management styles? Who is best suited to respond to these challenges?
2. What types of institutional incentives can be developed to encourage faculty and administrators to collaborate and share the power and responsibility they have been given?
3. What changes in the faculty reward system can increase involvement? Are these different for the quality or quantity of involvement? What is the price for increased shared authority?
4. Unions often work to create a "level playing field" among faculty in different disciplines and among administrators of similar rank. What impact would this have on a revised reward structure which values involvement?
5. What can higher education institutions and private businesses learn to share in terms of employee empowerment? Which of these are the most effective?

References

American Association of University Professors. (1966). *1966 statement on government of colleges and universities.* Washington, DC: American Association of University Professors.

American Council on Education. (1979). Responsibilities in the conduct of athletic programs: American Council on Education policy statements. *Educational Record,* 60 (4), 345-350.

Ardaiolo, F. (1993). Involving faculty with student affairs: Some personal pointers. *College Student Affairs Journal,* 13(1), 24-36.

Argyris, C. (1964). *Integrating the individual and the organization.* New York: Wiley.

Arnstein, S. A. (1976). A ladder of citizen participation. In E. Ingram and R. McIntosh (Eds.) *Adaptive Processes in Educational Organizations.* Edmonton: Department of Educational Administration, Faculty of Education, University of Alberta.

Association of American Colleges. (1985). *Integrity in the college curriculum.* Washington, DC: Association of American Colleges.

Astin, A. (1977). *Four critical years.* San Francisco: Jossey-Bass.

Astin, A. (1993). *What matters in college: Four critical years revisited.* San Francisco: Jossey-Bass.

Atwell, R. H. (1991). Sports reform: Where is the faculty? *Academe,* 77 (1), 10-12.

Bailey, W. (1988). Turnover in hospital fund raising: Asking the tough questions. *Fund Raising Management,* 3, 90-91.

Baldridge, J. V. (1982). Shared governance: A fable about the lost magic kingdom. *Academe,* 68(1), 12-15.

Bales, R. F., & Strodtbeck, F. L. (1951). Phases in group problem solving. *Journal of Abnormal and Social Psychology,* 46, 485-495.

Ballard v. Blount, 581 F. Supp. 160 (N. D. Ga. 1983).

Barr, M. J. (1997). New professionals institute address. National Association of Student Personnel Administrators Region IV-East New Professionals Institute, Chicago, IL.
Bennis, W. G., & Sheppard, H. A. (1956). A theory of group development. *Human Relations*, 9, 415-437.
Bergmann, B. (1991). Bloated administration, blighted campuses. *Academe*, 77(6), 12-16.
Bila, T. A. (1991). *Certified fund raising executives: Their profile and the approaches they have used to obtain their current employment.* Unpublished doctoral dissertation, Southern Illinois University at Carbondale.
Birnbaum, R. (1988). *How colleges work.* San Francisco: Jossey-Bass.
Birnbaum, R. (1991). The latent organizational functions of the academic senate: Why senates do not work but will not go away. In R. Birnbaum (Ed.), *Faculty in Governance: The Role of Senates and Joint Committees in Academic Decision Making. New Directions for Higher Education Report 75* (pp. 1-25). San Francisco: Jossey-Bass.
Blake, E. S. (1996). The yin and yang of student learning in college. *About Campus*, 1(4), 4-9.
Blumer, H. (1969). *Symbolic interactionism: Perspective and method.* Englewood Cliffs, NJ: Prentice-Hall.
Boyd, C. (1985). *Faculty participation in decision making: Necessity or luxury?* (ASHE/ERIC Report Number 8). Washington, DC: ASHE/ERIC and the George Washington University.
Boyer, E. (1990). *Scholarship reconsidered: Priorities of the professoriate.* Princeton, NJ: The Carnegie Foundation for the Advancement of Teaching.
Brandon, M. C. (1995). Employee communication: From nice to necessity. *Communication World*, 12(3), 20-22.
Brown, S. S. (1990). Strengthening ties to academic affairs. In Barr, M. J., and M. L. Upcraft (eds.), *New Futures for Student Affairs: Building a Vision for Professional Leadership and Practice* (pp. 239-269). San Francisco: Jossey-Bass.

Brubacher, J. (1989). *On the philosophy of higher education*. San Francisco: Jossey-Bass.

Chait, R. P., & Ford, A. T. (1982). *Beyond traditional tenure.* San Francisco: Jossey-Bass.

Chronicle of Higher Education Almanac Issue, 1996. (1996). Number of colleges by enrollment, fall 1994. Chronicle of Higher Education Almanac Issue, XLIII(1), 14.

Collier, K. (1988). *Integration and synthesis of literature to develop a prototypic process for program review.* Unpublished doctoral dissertation, Auburn University, Auburn, AL.

Connick v. Myers, 461 U. S. 137 (1983).

Connolly, M. S., & Blanchette, R. (1986). Understanding and predicting alumni giving behavior. In J. A. Dunn (Ed.) *Enhancing the Management of Fund Raising* (pp. 69-89). San Francisco: Jossey-Bass.

Cramer, J. (1986). Winning or learning? *Phi Delta Kappan*, 67(9), K1-K8.

Creswell, J. W., Wheeler, D. W., Seagren, A. T., Egly, N. J., & Beyer, K. D. (1990). *The academic chairperson's handbook.* Lincoln, NE: University of Nebraska.

Curry, B. (1992). *Instituting enduring innovations: Achieving continuity of change in higher education. New Directions in Higher Education.* San Francisco: Jossey-Bass.

Cyert, R. M. (1978). The management of universities of constant or decreasing size. *Public Administration Review*, 38(4), 344-349.

Dealy, F. X., Jr. (1990). *Win at any cost: The sell-out of college athletics.* Secaucus, NJ: Carol.

Dell, S. (1992). A communication-based theory of the glass ceiling: Rhetorical sensitivity and upward mobility within the technical organization. *IEEE Transactions on Professional Communication*, 35(4), 230-235.

Dickason, D. G. (1979). The future of college athletics. *Educational Record*, 60(4), 499-509.

Dunn, W. J. (1987). *Perceptions of selected academic administrators in Alabama concerning their role in varying institutions.* Unpublished doctoral dissertation, University of Alabama.

Education Commission of the States. (1992). *Faculty workload: State and system perspectives.* Denver, CO: Education Commission of the States, State Higher Education Executive Officers.

Ellsworth, J. B. (1997, October). Technology and change for the information age. Microsoft in Higher Education [Online]. Available HTTP: www.micorsoft.com/education/hed/vision.htm#involve.

Engstrom, C., Sedlacek, W., & McEwen, M. (1995). Faculty attitudes toward male revenue and nonrevenue student athletes. *Journal of College Student Development,* 36(3), 217-227.

Ervin, L., Saunders, S. A., & Gillis, H. L. (1984, Spring). The right direction but short of the mark: The NCAA's proposal 48. *The College Board Review,* 15-19.

Fiedler, F. E. (1964). A contingency model of leadership effectiveness. In L. Berkowitz (Ed.), *Advances in experimental social psychology* (pp. 149-190). New York: Academic Press.

Fisher, J. L. (1984). *Power of the presidency.* New York: American Council on Education.

Florida International University. (1997). http://www.fiu.edu/~time4chg/library/threesteps.html.

Gardner, J. (1996). Academic and student affairs. Presentation to the Council of Independent College Deans, Washington, DC.

Gilmour, J. E. (1991). Participative governance bodies in higher education: Report of a national study. In R. Birnbaum (Ed.), *Faculty in Governance: The role of Senate and Joint Committees in Academic Decision Making. New Directions for Higher Education Report 75* (pp. 27-40). San Francisco: Jossey-Bass.

Glenny, L. (1976). *Presidents confront reality: From edifice complex to university without walls.* San Francisco: Jossey-Bass.

Glickman, C., Gordon, S. P., & Ross-Gordon, J. M. (1995). *Supervision of instruction: A developmental approach.* Boston: Allyn and Bacon.

Goodsell, A. (1992). *Collaborative learning: A sourcebook for higher education.* University Park, PA: NCTLA.
Grant, C. H. B. (1979). Institutional autonomy and intercollegiate athletics. *Educational Record,* 60(4), 409-149.
Greenbrier Group. (1967). The Greenbrier report. *College and University Journal,* 6(1), 1-40.
Hanford, G. H. (1979). Controversies in college sports. *Educational Record,* 60(4), 351-366.
Harleston v. Jeffries, 115 S. Ct. 502, 503 (1994).
Herzberg, F. (1966). *Work and the nature of man.* New York: World Press.
Heuerman, J. N., & Spitaels-Genser, E. (Summer 1985). Mirror, mirror on the wall. *NAHD Journal,* 10-11.
Hoeflich, M. H. (1987). Prospects for college and university fund raising. *Academe,* 73(1), 30-32.
Holland, P. (1997). *Faculty motivations for giving to their employing institutions.* Unpublished doctoral dissertation, University of Alabama, Tuscaloosa, AL.
Hossler, D., & Bean, J. (1990). *The strategic management of college enrollments.* San Francisco: Jossey-Bass.
Jones, D., & Lovell, C. (1993). *Handbook on human assets: Record-keeping and analysis.* Boulder, CO: National Center for Higher Education Management Systems.
Jungnickel, P. W. (1990). Faculty issues: Research and scholarly activity. Presentation in the Department of Educational Administration, University of Nebraska-Lincoln.
Kameras, D. (1996). Teamsters cry foul over UPS team concept. *AFL-CIO News,* 41(4), 5.
Kanungo, R. N. (1992). Alienation and empowerment: Some ethical imperatives in business. *Journal of Business Ethics,* 11, 413-422.
Katz, D., & Kahn, R. L. (1966). *The social psychology of organizations.* New York: John Wiley & Sons.
Kaufman, H. (1971). *The limits of organizational change.* Tuscaloosa, AL: University of Alabama Press.
Keller, G. (1983). *Academic strategy: The management revolution in higher education.* Baltimore, MD: Johns Hopkins University Press.

Kerr, C. (1991). *The great transformation in higher education*. Albany, NY: State University of New York.

Knight Foundation Commission on Intercollegiate Athletics. (1991). *Keeping faith with the student-athlete: A new model for intercollegiate athletics*. Charlotte, NC: Author.

Knight Foundation Commission on Intercollegiate Athletics. (1992). *A solid start: A report on reform of intercollegiate athletics*. Charlotte, NC: Author.

Komarovsky, M. (1985). *Women in college: Shaping new feminine identifies*. New York: Basic Books.

Kreps, G. (1990). *Organizational communication: Theory and practice*. White Plains, NY: Longman.

Kuh, G. D., Douglas, K. B., Lund, J. P., & Ramin-Gyurnek, J. (1994). *Student learning outside the classroom: Transcending artificial boundaries. ASHE-ERIC Higher Education Report 8*. Washington, DC: ASHE/ERIC and George Washington University.

Kuh, G. D., Bean, J., Bradley, R., & Coomes, M. (1986). Contributions of student affairs journals to the college student research. *Journal of College Student Personnel, 27*, 292-304.

Kuh, G. D. (1996a). Guiding principles for creating seamless learning environments for undergraduates. *Journal of College Student Development, 37*(2), 135-148.

Kuh, G. D. (1996b). Some things we should forget. *About Campus, 1*(4), 10-15.

Kuhn, T. (1970). *The structure of scientific revolution* (2nd ed). Chicago, IL: University of Chicago Press.

Layzell, D., Lovell, C., & Gill, J. (1996). Developing faculty as an asset in a period of change and uncertainity. In *Integrating Research on Faculty Seeking New Ways to Communication about the Academic Life of Faculty* (pp. 93-108). Washington, DC: U. S. Department of Education.

Levine, A. (January 31, 1997). Higher education new status as a mature industry. *The Chronicle of Higher Education*, A 48.

Levy, B. R., & Cherry, R. L. (Eds.). (1996). *The NSFRE fundraising dictionary*. New York: John Wiley & Sons.

Lewis, G. (1975). Theodore Roosevelt's role in the 1905 football controversy. In E. F. Zeigler (Ed.), *A History of Physical Education and Sport in the United States and Canada* (pp. 202-217). Champaign, IL: Stipes.

Mallenyzer, B. J. (1990). Teacher empowerment: The discourse, meaning, and social actions of teachers. Paper presented at the Annual Conference of States on Inservice Education, Orlando, Florida (ERIC Document Reproduction Service Number ED 327 496).

McCarty, D. J., & Reyes, P. (1987). Organizational models of governance: Academic deans' decision making styles. *Journal of Teacher Education, 87,* 2-5.

McCormack, T. F. (1995). *A study of governance in higher education in the State of Alabama.* Unpublished doctoral dissertation, University of Alabama, Tuscaloosa, AL.

Miles, R. E. (1965). Human relations or human resources? *Harvard Business Review, 43*(4), 148-155.

Miles, A. S. (1997). *College law* (2nd ed.). Tuscaloosa, AL: Sevgo Press.

Miles, A. S. (1987). *College law.* Tuscaloosa, AL: Sevgo Press.

Miller, M. T. (1997A). Faculty governance leaders in higher education: Roles, beliefs, and skills. Paper Presented to the 20th Annual Meeting of the Eastern Educational Research Association, Hilton Head, South Carolina.

Miller, M. T. (1997B). The Faculty Forum: A case study in shared authority. *Resources in Education, 32*(3). ERIC Clearinghouse on Higher Education Reproduction Service Number ED 401 774.

Miller, M. T., & Seagren, A. T. (1993). Faculty leader perceptions of improving participation in higher education governance. *College Student Journal, 27,* 112-118.

Miller, M. T., McCormack, T. F., & Newman, R. E. (1996). Faculty involvement in governance: A comparison of two faculties. *Journal of Staff, Organization, and Professional Development, 13*(4), 269-276..

Miller, M. T., McCormack, T. F., Maddox, J. F., & Seagren, A. T. (1996). Faculty participation in governance at small and large universities: Implications for practice. *Planning and Changing, 27*(3/4), 180-190.

Mingle, J. R. (1981). *Challenges of retrenchment: Strategies for consolidating programs, cutting costs, and reallocating resources.* San Francisco: Jossey-Bass.

Minnesota State Board for Community Colleges v. Knight, 465 U. S. 271 (1984).

Minnesota State Board for Community Colleges, et al, v. Leon Knight, 465 U. S. 271, 79 L Ed 2d 299, 104 S Ct 1058 (1984).

Morgan, A., & Newell, L. (1981). Strategic planning at a small college: To be comprehensive or to be distinctive. *Planning for Higher Education, 9,* 29-33.

Munn, B. M. (1996). *Shall the university be controlled by the trustees, administrators or by faculty?* Unpublished manuscript, The University of Alabama, Tuscaloosa, AL.

Murphy, P. J. (1991). A collaborative approach to professional development. *Education Research and Perspectives, 18*(1), 59-65.

National Association of College and University Business Officers. (1992). *College and university business administration* (5th ed). Washington, DC: NACUBO.

National Association of Student Personnel Administrators. (1987). *A Perspective on Student Affairs. A statement issued on the 50th anniversary of the student personnel point of view.* Washington, DC: Author.

National Center for Education Statistics. (1996). *Integrating research on faculty: Seeking new ways to communicate about the academic life of faculty.* Washington, DC: U. S. Department of Education, Office of Educational Research and Improvement.

National Collegiate Athletic Association. (1996). *1996-1997 manual of the National Collegiate Athletic Association.* Overland Park, KS: Author.

Norton, R. W. (1978). Foundation of a communicator style construct. *Human Communication Research, 4*(2), 99-112.

Norton, R. W. (1983). *Communicator style: Theory, applications and measures.* Beverly Hills, CA: Sage.

Panas, J. (1988). *Born to raise.* Chicago: Pluribus Press.

Plater, W. M. (1995). Future work: Faculty time in the 21st century. *Change, 27*(3), 23-33.

Prince, R. A., & File, K. M. (1994). *The seven faces of philanthropy.* San Francisco: Jossey-Bass.

Rahim, M., & Blum, A. A. (Eds.). (1994). *Global perspectives on organizational conflict.* Westport, CT: Praeger.

Ratcliff, J. (1989). Getting the facts, analyzing the data, building the case for institutional distinctiveness. In B. Townsend (Ed.), *A Search for Institutional Distinctiveness* (pp. 45-57). *New Directions for Community Colleges Report Number 65.* San Francisco: Jossey-Bass.

Rowland, A. W. (Ed.). (1986). *Handbook of institutional advancement* (2nd ed). San Francisco: Jossey-Bass.

Schroeder, C. C., Nicholls, G. M., & Kuh, G. D. (1983). Exploring the rain forest: Testing assumptions about taking risks. In G. Kuh (ed.), *Understanding Student Affairs Organizations. New Directions for Student Services No. 23* (pp. 51-65). San Francisco: Jossey-Bass.

Seagren, A. T., & Miller, M. T. (Spring 1994). Caught in the middle: The pressures of chairing an instructional unit. *The Department Chair: A Newsletter for Academic Administrators,* 4(4), 2-3.

Seibold, D. R. (1992). Making meetings more successful: Plans, formats, and procedures for group problem solving. In R. S. Cathcart and L. A. Samovar (eds.), *Small Group Communication* (pp.178-191). Dubuque, IA: William C. Brown.

Senge, P. M. (1990). *The fifth discipline: The art and practice of the learning organization.* New York: Doubleday Currency.

Seymour, D. (1988). *Developing academic programs: The climate for innovation.* College Station, TX: ASHE.

Smith, D. G. (1982). The next step beyond student development: Becoming partners within our institutions. *NASPA Journal,* 24(2), 10-13.

Smith, S. B. (1996). Growth of foundation funding in Doctoral Universities I and II during a period of decreasing state appropriations. Paper presented at the Annual Meeting of the Association for the Study of Higher Education, Memphis, TN.

Smith, R. A. (1983). Preludes to the NCAA: Early failures

of faculty intercollegiate athletic control. *Research Quarterly for Exercise and Sport*, 54(4), 372-382.

Smith, T. B., & Weith, R. A. (1985). Value-added: The student affairs professional as promoter of intellectual development. *NASPA Journal*, 23(2), 19-24.

Sperber, M. (1990). College sports inc.: The athletic department vs. the university. *Phi Delta Kappan*, 72(2), K1-K12.

Southern Association of Colleges and Schools. (1996). *Criteria for accreditation*. Decatur, GA: Author.

Strohm, P. (1980). Toward an AAUP policy on evaluation of administrators. *Academe*, 66(8), 406-413.

Taylor, F. W. (1911). *Shop management*. New York: Harper & Brothers.

Taylor, F. W. (1967). *The principles of scientific management*. New York: W. W. Norton & Company.

Thelin, J. R., & Wiseman, L. L. (1989). *The old college try: Balancing academics and athletics in higher education*. Washington, DC: George Washington University.

Todd, C. E. (1965). *The perceived functions of the junior college academic dean in the improvement of instruction*. Unpublished doctoral dissertation, University of Alabama.

Toner, J. L. (1984, Spring). A statement of NCAA policy and intentions regarding proposal 48. *The College Board Review*, 13-15.

Townsend, B., Newell, L., & Wiese, M. (1992). *Creating distinctiveness: Lessons from uncommon colleges and universities. Higher Education Report Number 6*. Washington, DC: ASHE-ERIC.

Trow, M. (1990). The academic senate. *Liberal Education*, 76 (1), 23-27.

Tucker, A., & Bryan, R. A. (1988). *The academic dean, dove, dragon, and diplomat*. New York: American Council on Education/Macmillan Publishing.

Underwood, J. (1980, May 19). Student-athletes: The sham, the shame. *Sports Illustrated*, pp. 36-72.

Vacik, S. M. (1997). *Critical incidents impacting the role and development of the academic department chair, 1870 to 1925*. Unpublished doctoral dissertation, University of Alabama.

Vroom, V. H., & Yetton, P. W. (1973). *Leadership and decision making*. Pittsburgh: University of Pittsburgh Press.

Ward, M. S. (1934). *Philosophies of administration current in the deanship in American colleges and universities*. Carbondale, IL: Southern Illinois University.

Wagner, A., & Kemmerer, F. (1985). The economics of educational reform. *Economics of Education Review*, 4 (2), 111-121.

Weber, M. (1947). *The theory of social and economic organizations*. New York: Free Press.

Weick, K. E. (1979). *The social psychology of organizing* (2nd ed.). Reading, MA: Addison-Wesley.

Westerfield, R. C. (1997). *Personal communication*. Tuscaloosa, AL: University of Alabama.

Williams, D., Gore, W., Broches, C., & Lostoski, C. (1987). One faculty's perceptions of its governance role. *Journal of Higher Education*, 58(6), 629-655.

Weistart, J. C. (1987). College sports reform: Where are the faculty? *Academe*, 73(4), 12-17.

Wood, L., & Wilson, R. C. (1972). Teachers with impact. *Research Reporter*, 7(2), 1-4.

Young, A. (1981). *Understanding accreditation*. San Francisco: Jossey-Bass.

Zemsky, R. (1996). The impact of higher education's new climate on faculty perceptions. In *Integrating Research on Faculty: Seeking New Ways to Communicate About the Academic Life of Faculty* (pp. 81-91). Washington, DC: Office of Educational Research and Improvement, U. S. Department of Education.

Zingg, P. J. (1982). Advising the student-athlete. *Educational Record*, 63(2), 16-19.

Zingg, P. J. (1983). No simple solution: Proposition 48 and the possibilities of reform. *Educational Record*, 64(3), 6-12.

Appendices

Appendix 1

Letter of Faculty Appointment

Dr. New Graduate
123 Dissertation Blvd.
College Town, USA

Dear Dr. Graduate:

I am pleased to have the opportunity of inviting you accept a tenure-earning appointment as Assistant Professor in the Special Education Program in the College of Education. This position will become effective on August 15, the beginning of the academic year, for an academic year salary of $34,000.

Under the provisions of The University Faculty Handbook, a final decision on awarding you tenure must be made no later than the sixth year of your service at The University. This will place mandatory consideration of tenure for you during the 19__-19__ academic year. College and University procedures call for a review of each untenured faculty member's performance during each year prior to mandatory tenure decision time. Decisions for promotion and/or tenure will be based heavily on your production of scholarly research and publication.

In your position your responsibilities could include, but may not be limited to the following:

1. Teaching courses in your areas of expertise. As the need arises, these course assignments may be taught on-campus or off-campus, including the international offerings;

2. Assisting in the development and implementation of programs for students;

3. Assisting in conducting and directing research;

4. Serving on graduate students' committees and assisting them with their research efforts;

5. Advising students in your area;

6. Serving as a consultant, with administrative approval, to public and private organizations and agencies appropriate to your expertise.

Also, you would be responsible for developing a personal scholarship program that will result in scholarly research and publication.

I hope you understand that I must have someone to serve in this position at the beginning of the academic year. Therefore, if I have not received your letter of acceptance by July 15, I will assume you are not interested in this offer and will extend the invitation to another candidate.

It would please us if you would give this offer your favorable consideration. I would appreciate hearing from you, in writing, as soon as possible regarding your decision.

Sincerely,

College Dean

c: Budget Officer
　 Provost
　 Department Chair

Appendix 2

Listing of Institutional Committees*

Membership Recommended by Committee on Committees

    Academic Advising Committee
    Awards Committee
    Campus Master Plan Committee
    Campus Security and Safety Committee
    Committee on University Committees
    Energy Management Committee
    Equal Opportunity Committee
    Faculty and Staff Benefits Committee
    International Students and Scholars Committee
    International Studies Committee
    Maintenance Personnel Committee
    Office/Clerical/Technical Staff Committee
    Parking and Traffic Regulations Committee
    Professional Staff Committee
    Recreation Committee
    Resources and Priorities Committee
    Staff Development Committee
    Student Development Committee
    Student Health Committee
    Student Life Committee
    Supply Store Committee
    Teaching and Learning Committee
    Undergraduate Admissions and Retention Committee
    University Plans Committee

Membership Appointed by President, Elected, or Composed by Other Means

    Academics and Athletics Committee
    Biosafety Research Committee
    Conflict of Interest Policy Committee
    Cooperative Education Committee
    Core Curriculum Oversight Committee

Faculty Participation in the Selection of Deans
and Department Chairpersons and in the Evaluation
of Academic Programs Committee
Financial Aid Committee
Graduate Scholarship Committee
Health and Safety Committee
Health Professions Committee
Information Technology Committee
Institutional Animal Care and Use Committee
Institutional Review Board for Protection of Human
Subjects
Intercollegiate Athletics Committee
Media Planning Board
Mediation Committee
Radiation Control Committee
Research Advisory Committee
ROTC Programs Review Committee
University Press Committee
Waste Reduction and Recycling Committee

Councils and Committees which Support Standing Committees

Council of Assistant and Associate Deans
Council of Deans
Graduate Council
Honors Council
Human Relations Council
Interim (Pre-Summer Session) Coordinating Council
Teacher Education Council

Other Working Groups

Merger or Discontinuance of Academic Units
Committee
Faculty Senate

*Adapted from the listing of councils and committees of The University of Alabama, Tuscaloosa, Alabama.

Appendix 3

Sample Administrator Rating

The Administrator Appraisal Program is directed by Faculty Senate, with support and implementation by the Center for Teaching and Learning in the Division of Student Affairs. Designed to foster quality academic administration on campus and to encourage administrators to be responsive to faculty concerns.

The Appraisal Program invites faculty members to rate and comment on the performance of campus, system, and college administrators, then distributes results to faculty members, administrators, their supervisors, and the public. This program is loosely modelled after the Faculty Classroom Student Opinion Survey program, where students rate and comment on courses and instructors.

All responses are anonymous. The forms are handled only by staff of the Division of Student Affairs and the Center for Teaching and Learning.

The form asks for ratings of the administrator's performance and invites narrative comments on the administrators listed. Average ratings for each administrator are publicly released. The narrative comments are transcribed and sent only to the individual administrator. They are not otherwise released.

Positions evaluated— Schools, colleges, and libraries: deans, associate and assistant deans; associate directors of libraries. Evaluated by faculty in the unit only. Campus-wide: chancellor; vice chancellor for academic affairs; associate and assistant vice chancellors; dean and associate dean of the graduate school; dean of libraries.

Results for the item "overall administrative performance"

Administrator Title	% of N (N)	A	B	C	D	F	1997	1996
Name 1 President	27% (1997 n=314; 1996 n=117)	43	39	11	3	4	3.14 B	3.21 B
Name 2 Vice President for Acad Affairs	11% (1997 n=130; 1996 n=25)	39	35	12	5	8	2.93 B	2.32 C+

Name 3   31%   19 29 24 15 13   2.28 C+ 2.81 B
Assc VP Acad Affairs (1997 n=365; 1996 n=202)

Name 4   21%   13 21 32 17 18   1.94 C 2.24 C
Asst V Acad Affairs (1997 n=248; 1996 n=143)

Name 5   18%   14 36 25 12 13   2.26 C+ 2.22 C
Vice Pres for Student Affairs (1997 n=208; 1996 n=105)

Name 6   20%   12 22 30 20 17   1.92 C 2.28 C+
Diversity Affairs (1997 n=239; 1996 n=151)

* Average rating on the item "overall administrative performance." Scale: "very poor" (F=0) to "very good" (A=4).

** 1996 Average Rating not strictly comparable to 1997 ratings because the form and questions changed.

Appendix 4

Pyramid Concept of Academic Alumni Giving

	Major and Deferred Gifts	Key Volunteers
Touchstone of institutional quality	Leadership Gifts	Sense of Power Institutional Ideals
Living Endowment	Larger Gift	Experienced volunteers; Ownership and Achievement
	Regular Gifts	
Source of Current Funds	A Gift Defining a Base	Entry level volunteers; tasks; Sense of Affiliation

| Philosophical | Operational | Psychological |

Author Notes

Todd Adams is the Coordinator of Greek Life in the Office of the Dean of Students at The University of Toledo. He holds an M.S. in College Student Personnel from Southern Illinois University at Carbondale, and has published and researched in the areas of student leadership development and Greek life.

Jane G. Bartee is a Graduate Assistant with the University of Alabama Women's Swimming Team. She was a seven-time All-American and three time Academic All-American swimmer for the University of Nebraska-Lincoln, and is currently pursing graduate work in Higher Education Administration at the University of Alabama. She also serves as a Research Associate for the National Data Base on Faculty Involvement in Governance.

Dr. Thomas A. Bila is a senior partner in the firm of Coffey, Bila, and Associates in Omaha, Nebraska. He is the former Director of Development at Western New England College, he holds bachelors and masters degrees from the University of Detroit and a Ph.D. in Higher Education Administration from Southern Illinois University. He has previously served as the Executive Director of the Rockford Memorial Hospital Foundation and the Director of Special, Major, and Annual Gifts at the Southern Illinois University Foundation. Dr. Bila also holds a CFRE offered through the National Society of Fund Raising Executives.

Dr. Exir Brennen is the Director of Institutional Research and Planning at Alabama A & M University in Huntsville, Alabama. She has previously served as an Institutional Research Officer at The University of Alabama, where she also earned a Ph.D. in Higher Education Administration. She conducts research and studies the role of institutional effectiveness within the context of higher education change.

Dr. Jennifer P. Evans is the Director of Educational Services with CareCentric Solutions in Atlanta, Georgia. She is a former Assistant Professor of Educational Leadership at The University of Alabama, holds her Ph.D. in Educational Leadership from the same institution, and has over a decade of experience working in private sector human resource management and corporate training with Panasonic.

Dr. Thomas F. McCormack is Vice President for Academics and Dean of the College at Marion Military Institute in Marion, Alabama. A retired United States Air Force Colonel, he holds a Ph.D. in Higher Education Administration from The University of Alabama where he also serves as an adjunct faculty member and Senior Research Associate with the National Data Base on Faculty Involvement in Governance.

Dr. Michael T. Miller is an Associate Professor and Chair of the Higher Education Administration Program at The University of Alabama. He holds an Ed.D. from the University of Nebraska-Lincoln, and currently serves as Director of the National Data Base on Faculty Involvement in Governance. He has previously served as the Director of the Nebraska Research and Development Unit on Vocational Education and as the Director of Annual Giving for the Southern Illinois University Foundation.

Dr. Richard E. Newman is an Associate Professor and Chair of the Department of Physical Education at Presbyterian College in South Carolina. He previously served as an Assistant Professor of Health and Physical Education at the University of Arkansas-Monticello. He holds an Ed.D. from the University of Nebraska-Lincoln, and has spent over 20 years as a college level football coach at such institutions as Pacific University, the University of Mary, Western State College, and the University of Northern Colorado.

Dr. Kathleen Randall is the Associate Vice President for Student Affairs, Director of Student Life, and Assistant Professor of Higher Education Administration at The University of Alabama. She has over 20 years experience at all levels of student affairs administration, and has consistently published in such areas as Greek life, undergraduate involvement, diversity, and administrative performance. She holds a Ph.D. from The University of Alabama.

www.ingramcontent.com/pod-product-compliance
Lightning Source LLC
Chambersburg PA
CBHW071204160426
43196CB00011B/2190